Tonguebreaker

Tonguebreaker

poems and performance texts

Leah Lakshmi
Piepzna-Samarasinha

ARSENAL PULP PRESS
VANCOUVER

TONGUEBREAKER
Copyright © 2019 by Leah Lakshmi Piepzna-Samarasinha

ARSENAL PULP PRESS
Suite 202 – 211 East Georgia St.
Vancouver, BC V6A 1Z6
Canada
arsenalpulp.com

The publisher gratefully acknowledges the support of the Canada Council for the Arts and the British Columbia Arts Council for its publishing program, and the Government of Canada, and the Government of British Columbia (through the Book Publishing Tax Credit Program), for its publishing activities.

Arsenal Pulp Press acknowledges the xʷməθkʷəy̓əm (Musqueam), Sḵwx̱wú7mesh (Squamish), and səl̓ilwətaʔɬ (Tsleil-Waututh) Nations, speakers of Hul'q'umi'num'/Halq'eméylem/hən̓q̓əmin̓əm̓ and custodians of the traditional, ancestral, and unceded territories where our office is located. We pay respect to their histories, traditions, and continuous living cultures and commit to accountability, respectful relations, and friendship.

Cover and text design by Oliver McPartlin
Cover illustration by Shayda Kafai
Edited by Meg Day
Copy edited by Shirarose Wilensky
Proofread by Alison Strobel

Printed and bound in Canada

Library and Archives Canada Cataloguing in Publication:
Piepzna-Samarasinha, Leah Lakshmi, 1975–, author
      Tonguebreaker / Leah Lakshmi Piepzna-Samarasinha.
Poems.
Issued also in print and electronic formats.
ISBN 978-1-55152-757-4 (softcover).–ISBN 978-1-55152-758-1
(HTML)
      I. Title. II. Title: Tongue breaker.

PS8631.I46T66 2019   C811'.6   C2018-906220-7

                                      C2018-906221-5

For Jesse Manuel, forever.

and for Taueret, Bryn, Basil, Jerika, Amanda and Emma,
and all femmes in struggle.

And what do we know about the resurrected femme body? What do we know about the divine?
—Amber Dawn, "Corpus"

In the day-to-day femme functions as a dare, a longing, and a political decision about how to move in the world ... Femme smiles while looking at me dead in the eye saying: *I dare you to join me in doing all we can to get free and get to that other world we have one foot in, while leaving no parts of our beautiful selves behind.*
—Jess St. Louis

Autism: takiwātanga—his or her own time and space.
Disabled: whaikaha—to have strength, to have ability, otherly abled, enabled.
—Keri Opai, *Te Reo Hāpai: The Language of Enrichment*

You know it has to have been an autistic person who invented fire. Who else would just keep trying and trying to make it work, until it did?
—Cyree Jarelle Johnson

Contents

Thanks and acknowledgments

This book was written as an immigrant on occupied Duwamish, Lenape, and Huron-Wendat, Mississauga of New Credit and Anishinaabe land, bound by treaty law including the Treaty of Point Elliott, Great Law of Peace, the Dish With One Spoon and Two Row Wampum covenants.

"Femme houses," "Riches," "Bad road" and "Adaptive device" first appeared in *The Deaf Poets Society* (August 2016, October 2016). "Crip magic spells," "Crip fairy godmother" and "All the femmes comes back" were commissioned, written and performed as part of Sins Invalid's October 2016 performance at ODC Theater, San Francisco, CA. "Crip fairy godmother" and "Femme futures" were published in *Hematopoiesis*, Issue 2: Infection, summer 2017. "All the femmes come back" was published in *Femmescapes*, Volume 3, fall 2017. "Cripstory" was commissioned by the Paul K. Longmore Institute of San Francisco State University as part of their *Patient No More* exhibit, which launched in fall 2016, commemorating the Section 504 direct actions. "Crip infinity" appeared in *Anomaly: Glitterbrain*, fall 2017. "3 crazy queens" was written for and performed at To Exist Is to Resist: Sick and Disabled QT/BIPOC Ancestors and Futures, Gay City Arts, Seattle, January 2018.

"Crip fairy godmother" contains an extended quote from *Parable of the Sower* by Octavia Butler. "Crip infinity" contains echotextia, an autistic poetic form where others' words echo in our own and are in conversation. My line "What do we know of the crip body?" is echotextia of Amber Dawn's "What do we know of the queer femme body?" from her poem "Corpus."

Thank you to Leanne Betasamosake Simpson, for writing *This Accident of Being Lost* and inspiring this book's form and content with your Indigenous decolonial queer poetics. Thanks to Cyree Jarelle Johnson for their earliest wise eyes on this book, which helped me tear up and rewrite it. Thank you to Femme Force Four, a.k.a. Amber Dawn, Kama La Mackerel and Kai Cheng Thom, for coming together and reminding me of the sacred joy and work of femme poetry ceremony. Thank you to Sins Invalid for existing and for inviting me to create work for our 2016 show, and in particular to Neve Mazique and Nomy Lamm, for being the creative collaboration that helped me write "Crip fairy godmother," "Crip magic spells" and "All the femmes come back." Thank you to *Deaf Poets Society*, *Anomaly* and *Hematopoiesis* for creating new sites of disability justice literary community, and to the cast and crew of To Exist Is to Resist, Kindling Love and Adept, for creating disabled creative space in Seattle. Thank you to all my gifted writing students in Hard Femme Poetics and Frida and Harriet's Children. All of these spaces were the container that allowed those words to be written.

Thanks to Billie Rain, Neve Mazique, Stacey Milbern, Gesig Selena Isaac, Syrus Marcus Ware, Lisa Amin, TextaQueen, Jonah Aline Daniel, Cyree Jarelle Johnson, Setareh Mohammad, Chanelle Gallant, Ejeris Dixon, Tina Zavitsanos, Aaron Ambrose, E.T. Russian, Meg Day, Aruna Zehra, Mackenzie Reynolds and Amirah Mizrahi. Thank you to the global sick and disabled queer and trans Black, Indigenous and brown communities, to the femmes, care workers, poets, survivors and every Central Mass sick and disabled femme ever. There's no one I'd rather live through the end of the world with than you.

Jesse, this is already dedicated to you, but thank you, for every part of this breaking broken light.

Preface:
the epistemology of breaking/
how you make a book

This book is a magic spell about what it means to be surrounded by death and live on.

Being surrounded by death and persisting is a disabled knowledge. It is a femme knowledge. It is a knowledge held in Black, brown and Indigenous bodies.

This book's origins are a funny femme of color disabled working class creation story. Like many (working class) writers, I hustle whatever state granting apparatus I have access to as social assistance to help me pay my rent while I write. Toronto Arts Council, Ontario Arts Council and (a tiny bit) Canada Council writing grants helped me immeasurably when I was an emerging writer who was chronically ill, brown, nuts and poor; those injections of a couple thousand dollars here and there saved my ass, got me out of overdraft and bought groceries and time to be a weirdo in front of a computer with the words. Those arts councils have come through less in the past five years, with increasing austerity (they ask me to sit on grant juries now but won't give me money), but they saved me in my twenties and into my thirties.

So, it was the fall of 2014, my book of poetry *Bodymap* was at the publisher going through edits, I was incredibly broke because the three work gigs I had counted on had all flaked, and I looked at the Canada Council website and went, *I've won some awards, I'm a "mid-career" writer, maybe I'll write a big fancy proposal and get some cash so I can pay rent while I write the next one.* It was the first book of poetry I conceived of that wasn't going to just be "everything I've written over the past 3 to 5 years smashed together into a book." Nope—I had gotten fascinated by the graffiti poems etched into the walls of Sigiriya—an ancient castle in Sri Lanka overrun with poems written in Sinhalese, Tamil and Sanskrit of the mudaliyar's love for all the women he boned, including ancient sex workers. And I was going to write a fancy grant to go to Sri Lanka, study the poems and write my own femme on femme poetry book—while also grappling with how "untranslatable/ unpronounceable" Sri Lankan names and femme of color disabled bodies are, and how our long-ass complexities are a form of resistance. The title came to me first: *Tonguebreaker*.

Good idea. Unfortunately, it turned out to be pretty "untranslatable" to the couple of grant juries I submitted it to, and I got turned down for the money. I shelved the idea. Maybe I would eventually save enough money for the $2,000 plane ticket and do the book on my own.

In the meantime, life kept happening. In 2015, Taueret Davis, beloved Black queer fat femme artist, educator and community icon, killed herself, sending shock waves of grief, terror and despair through femme communities. A two-year period (which isn't necessarily over) I think of as "the femme suicide years" commenced, where other beloved femme writers living at the intersections of multiple margins—Bryn Kelly, Amanda Arkansassy Harris, Basil Arbogast and Jerika Bolen (as well as more femmes I don't know)—killed themselves. Many other people were privately suicidal. 2016 felt like a marathon of intensity as many beloved and complex public figures, from Prince to Fidel Castro and Carrie Fisher, died. It felt like they were rushing to get the hell out of here and become ancestors. Relentless, brutal murders of Black people, trans women of color, Indigenous folks and brown folks happened and we were unsure if the killing would ever stop.

Then, Trump got elected after his campaign pumped up fascist hatred across North America. Things became even more apocalyptic as his presidency ushered in open fascism and attacks on Black and brown people, Indigenous land, disabled and sick people, immigrants and undocumented folks. Things felt too much to bear, and then there was more to bear, and more.

And: I fell in love with another chronically ill, working class femme of color survivor, and was transformed by that love. I moved across the continent and in with them. I released the trauma survival memoir I'd worked on for a decade, and got transformed and shook by the process. I started my first non-independent-contractor job in a decade, and quit when its racism and ableism made me sick. I was surrounded by both the peace, quiet and green of the Pacific Northwest, and the creep of its white liberal and fascist violence. My mom started to die and I got hit by grief so hard it knocked me to my knees. I had the space to recognize how some relationships I'd thought of as "complicated" were actually emotionally abusive. I found my no. I came out as autistic/neurodivergent. Sins Invalid, the disability justice performance collective I am lucky to be a part of, curated our first show in four years, on crip life cycles, birthing, living and dying crip wisdom.

I wrote about all that. Because that is the writer's job. Somewhere towards the end, I remembered on the toilet one day that I had written a bunch of pretty big performance texts when I was codirecting and performing with Mangos With Chili. Texts that were, mostly, about disabled queer of color literary ancestors and my relationship to them. I figured they were part of the work, too.

This book is not what I intended it to be, but it is the book that needed it be written, and a map of the wending, winding creative process of being a working class, disabled femme of color artist who is awake, living and noticing, in these times.

At Amanda's memorial, white working class femme liturgist Blyth Barnow talked about the Japanese cultural practice of kintsugi, of loving what is imperfect and decorating it with gold. She wrote:

> I heard it referred to as a "philosophy not of replacement, but of awe, reverence, and restoration." It is an ancient practice. A spiritual practice.
>
> And, for me, there is something very Femme about all of it. The idea that adornment is a form of reverence, of binding

together. The notion that our cracks, our wounds, can be beautiful too. So much femme labor, femme love, comes from that place of breaking. It is what teaches us how to see each other. It is what teaches us how to see you. And in learning how to heal we have also learned how to mend. We take what is supposed to go unseen and amplify it, make it too much, put gold on it.

And the tricky part is that sometimes we adorn it because we understand that beauty is powerful, and sometimes we adorn it because we don't believe anyone would look at us otherwise. That if we are too raw or too wounded or too messy, we will lose our place in community. Sometimes we think we have to be finished healing before we can be worthy.

To me, this is also a disabled practice. What are we as disabled people if not people in a practice of learning to love and/or learn our brilliant imperfection (as Eli Clare coined it)? Our brokenbeautiful, as Alexis Pauline Gumbs wrote it?

Living through femme death as a disabled femme of color whose work is to sit with, understand and undo my suicidal ideation has pushed me harder to imagine our futures. We are the ones who are called on to do our work to fuck shit up, live with joy, live with pain, come out the other side, find another side after that. So often we think we have to wait 'til we are healed, that we are too fucked up to do this.

But this is our task, with all our radiant imperfect broken: to remake the world and create our futures.

1. femme futures

Femme futures

Where does the future live in your body?
Touch it

1.
Sri Lankan radical women never come alone.
We have a tradition of coming in groups of three or four, minimum.
The Thiranagama sisters are the most famous and beloved,
but in the '20s my appamma and great-aunties were the Wild Alvis Girls.
Then there's your sister, your cousin, your great-aunties
everyone infamous and unknown.
We come in packs   we argue
we sneak each other out of the house
we have passionate agreements and disagreements
we love each other very much but can't stand to be in the same room or
    continent for years.
We do things like, oh, start the first rape crisis center in Jaffna in a war zone
in someone's living room with no funding.
When war forces our hands,
we all move to Australia or London or Thunder Bay together
or, if the border does not love us, we are what keeps Skype in business.
When one or more of us is murdered
by the state or a husband
we survive
whether we want to or not.

I am an only child
I may not have been born into siblinghood
but I went out and found mine

Made mine.

We come in packs
even when we are alone

Because sometimes the only ancestral sisterlove waiting for you
is people in books, dreams
aunties you made up
people waiting for you in the clouds ten years in the future
and when you get there
you make your pack
and you send that love
back.

2.
When the newly disabled come
they come bearing terror and desperate. Everyone else has left them
to drown on the Titanic. They don't know that there is anyone
but the abled. They come asking for knowledge
that is common to me as breath, and exotic to them as, well,
being disabled and not hating yourself.
They ask about steroids and sleep. About asking for help.
About how they will ever possibly convince their friends and family
they are not lazy and useless.
I am generous—we crips always are.
They *were* me.
They don't know if they can call themselves *that*,
they would never use *that word*, but they see me calling myself *that*,
i.e., disabled, and the lens is blurring, maybe there is another world
they have never seen

where crips limp slowly, laugh, have shitty and good days
recalibrate the world to our bodies instead of sprinting trying to keep up.
Make everyone slow down to keep pace with us.

Sometimes, when I'm about to email the resource list,
the interpreter phone numbers, the hot chronic pain tips, the best place to
    rent a ramp,
my top five favorite medical cannabis strains, my extra dermal lidocaine
patch—*it's about to expire, but don't worry, it's still good*—I want to slip in a
    P.S. that says,
remember back when I was a crip
and you weren't, how I had a flare and had to cancel our day trip
and when I told you, you looked confused
and all you knew how to say was, Boooooooooo!
as I was lying on the ground trying to breathe?
Do you even remember that?
Do your friends say that to you now?
Do you want to come join us, on the other side?
Is there a free future in this femme of color disabled body?

3.
When I hear my femme say, *When I'm old and riding a motorcycle with*
    white hair down my back.
When I hear my femme say, *When I'm old and sex work paid off my house*
    and my retirement.
When I hear my femme/myself say, *When I get dementia and I am held*
    with respect when I am between all worlds.
When I see my femme packing it all in, because crip years are like dog
    years and you never know when they're going to shoot Old Yeller.

When I hear my femme say, *when I quit my teaching gig and never have to deal with white male academic nonsense again.*

When I hear us plan the wheelchair accessible femme of color trailer park,
the land we already have a plan to pay the taxes on
See the money in the bank and the ways we grip our thighs back to ourselves

When I hear us dream our futures,
believe we will make it to one,
We will make one.

The future lives in our bodies
Touch it.

Crip fairy godmother

Hi, baby crip
I know, you feel like a ton of bricks just hit you. They did.
But I'm your crip fairy godmother
and I'm here to tell you what's going to happen.
I hate to say it, but it's a cheat sheet called, they mostly don't care about us

Because this is exactly what's going to happen:
Your able-bodied friends will stop calling.
It's going to be real cute for a minute,
but then there will be other things to look at on Instagram
They're going to wish you a "speedy recovery"
and they will be so surprised when there is neither
speed   or a recovery.
They will say, "oh, you're not disabled, sweetie, don't call yourself that."
They will laugh uncomfortably when you state simple facts about your
    body
They will tell you to hurry up
every way they can
with every deep sigh, every *it's fine*,
every time they'll walk ahead of you so fast
they don't even notice you're gone.
There will be expectations of gratitude!
There will be, "Hope you feel better soon!"

Most of all there's this:
they will forget you
You have to know this, they will forget you,
over and over again.

They will forget you use a chair   They will forget you use a cane.
They will forget you think in flowers   They will forget that you're Deaf,
and they will think they're doing you a favor
by forgetting your disability
because that means you get to be human, like them.
If they can't forget these things
they are going to forget
that you exist.

They're gonna take your sick personally
I mean very personally   I mean you are in a wheelchair *at* them,
I mean you are puking and shitting for hours *at* them,
I mean you *did this*, by which I mean, you got disabled, to get at them
because they, the abled, are the center of the world
and when you continue to exist
you're gonna be a rip in the fabric of their universe.
You're going to give a shit about things you never cared about before
and they're going to be so grateful
they aren't you

They will stop calling
They will care about you but not other disabled people because we are still
    losers
They will have absolutely no idea of the hurt they cause with every syllable
but you will.

I know this sucks
but I'm your crip fairy godmother and I'm here to give you some important
    information straight
This is not in any pamphlet the hospital will send you home with

Its operating instructions. I mean to save your life
with what I was taught in the secret guild of other sickos
with what I learned the hard way

Dear baby crip,
it's not all bad news,
because here's what's also going to happen
It's a magic spell I'm calling into existence
It's Defense against the White Able-Bodied Arts time!
This is crip Hogwarts with none of the racism or heteronormativity!
This is all our lightning scars on our foreheads glowing, not just one special
    white boy's!

Because here's what's also going to happen,
after they leave
after nothing   and everything
happens on your rebel body's schedule
You will discover
that you
do
not
give
a fuck.
You will discover that they bore the hell out of you
right next to them breaking your heart.

It will probably take you years
to begin to maybe not hate yourself
but I invoke that you will
This is a magic spell,

because we write the future with our bodies every day
that you make it
and make more than you could imagine
You will gain a wild pack of crips
sharing vicodin, hearing aid hookups, favorite terps, the shared ramp
the inside scoop on the lexapro, the link to the beloved breathing mask.

You will drool   type   stim   limp
and shake with joy
I invoke that you will move as slow and weird as you want
and others will roll and limp with you in a wild pack of slowness

You will gain skill in learning to not predict the future
You will learn every magic trick
to shape-shift pain
You become an alchemist
and you are better than
any of the most boring neurotypicals in the world

Didn't Lauren Olamina, that crip, say:

All successful life is
Adaptable,
Opportunistic,
Tenacious,
Interconnected, and
Fecund.
Understand this.
Use it.

Shape God.[1]

Shape god
You, you are god

Disability is adaptive, interconnected, tenacious, voracious, slutty, silent,
   raging,
life giving

We are crip Earthseed
but we are not going anywhere
You are not an individual health defect
You are a systemic war battalion
You come from somewhere
You are a we
We know shit they'll need to know
We know shit they have no idea of
We have survived a million things they said would kill us
We prove them all wrong
Even death is different here
not a failure
but a glittery cosmos.

What can I do?

I can breathe sky into the spaces of my spasming spine
I can eat Fritos and watch an entire series on Netflix with no shame
I organize my whole community without ever leaving my bed

---

1 Octavia Butler, "Earthseed: Book of the Living, verse 19," *Parable of the Sower* (New York: Four Walls Eight Windows, 1993).

I can show you how to make a ramp out of some styrofoam and a hot dog
I can run a million miles a second panic attack wired for sound
I am a hyperempath like Lauren Olamina
I can run this whole show tapping emails on my phone with my forehead
I can jump off a bridge and not fall
I regrow my neural pathways into the future
I XFemme
I can survive
I bliss
I can make sure we all make it
I can see my vulnerability
not as a crime

So tell me.

What
can you do?
What
are the magic tricks
you will teach me
that I don't even know yet,
that will be
what saves
my life

For Maya Chinchilla

Riches: Oakland 2010–2013

Oakland, summer 2010 or 2013, pre- or early apocalypse. Walking slowly on your crip parking pass and cane to that big Target on the Shellmound in West O. Limping in with all the other three hustles, waiting on food stamps, crazy and not eligible for state disability or making state disability stretch folks. The chin-nod smiles to the other cane-using walkies and the chair users, people who clearly wet-wiped themselves down because the shower was just too much, people who've been crying all day. Just like you.

You find yourselves here. Not at a community center run by the state or anarchists or an eager social justice nonprofit. Your community center is all of you shopping the dollar section. Hoodie and scarf and leggings and vest ready to take-on-take-off, Oakland hot-cold, your cloth shopping bag full of special rocks and pain meds and tinctures and snacks and water, ready as you can be for any possible way your bodymind might fall apart.

After, you'll drive to one of the many free parks with spectacular nature to your east coast eyes—*redwoods?*—or the pull-off at 60th past the 80 to sit and watch the Bay. The cops won't show up unless it's after 10 p.m. or someone's drunk. No matter how fucked up your car is, how the registration's overdue from last year and you've got six unpaid parking tickets you can't pay so they're gonna triple, that view of Mt. Tam and the big real ocean makes you rich. Seeing other brown disabled poor people around you makes you rich.

Your car's full of old coffee cups and mason jars, the rained-on-for-twenty-years leather ragtop is molding and flaking from the inside. But it's your palace. You can haul anything—free furniture you notice on Bay Area Queer Exchange when you're working from home and trying to be productive while your belly hurts and breakfast takes two hours because all your roommates want to talk (after all, aren't you always home?), all the snacks for the show, tons of nettles you pick for free at the secret spot near Muir Creek, your friend's manual wheelchair, all the performers back to Oakland after Sins (even though Aurora has to hang her head out the window the whole way because the mold is so intense). All these places, they are rich. Four queer of color krip artists doing a show about sex and disability, getting paid, driving home late together? Riches. Lucky.

You're still broke as hell and worry about money constantly, but you always have been. And right now, you feel rich, even with that worry. You've got enough for food and your $175 rent, gas at the cheap place on San Pablo, community acupuncture at the $10 spot, Arizmendi pizza crumpled tinfoil wrappers. Pretty is easier here than so many places; you can just look outside. Your hips hurt less because there's no snow, you can get high-CBD weed from Harborside and a free Reiki treatment while they bag it up. Your bank account reads $435, $127, -$97, sometimes $1,178 for a second before you pay rent and credit card minimums and student loans. But you have time. Time to write, time to drive your friend to work or acu. Time to have a meeting and another meeting. Time to be a disabled queer brown artist.

Eventually, you will realize that all your smart-ass strategies that make you feel like a baller still don't pay anything close to what other people consider enough. But right now, you feel like you've figured out the secret.

There's fear. Always. The feeling in your gut of waiting on the check, walking to the mailbox, emailing to follow up, again, what happens when there's some fuckup and the money you were counting on doesn't show up for months— *eight months one time*—and some abled money person is so casual about it.

It's hard for you to explain yourselves to the abled and monied. They figure you must have a trust fund or a rich parent to be able to do all these things.

Be sick and say it out loud. Not have a 9-to-5. Write. How do you explain, you're just broke, always been? You don't call yourself poor, because you are so clear you're not working at Walmart or cutting hair in Worcester like your cousins. You always feel lucky, so lucky, just to be able to breathe. And just regular, regular. Poor folks you know don't call ourselves poor, we're just regular. Artists are supposed to be special snowflakes anointed by god, but there's this other way, the way you were taught, that we are ordinary, on the bus, falling apart. Especially when we're spending hours of our days on the toilet, making a movie with all your krip friends on your couch, too sick to work, laughing, writing a poem on your phone as your ass squeezes out more IBS. But you don't have access to so much able-bodied folks who aren't nuts can grab. All that little bit of extra art money went right to the therapy that stops your millionth suicidal ideation from working, that allows you to lurch back from pain, from another pneumonia.

It's hard to explain lifelong disability and insanity to people whose ableism makes them unable to see yours no matter how often you blow your spoons explaining it.

You look back at all those years of early 20s crazy girl hermit life, $425 apartment life, weird brain, hustle, three days' peace with the landline pulled out the wall, walking silent, writing poems on your Mac classic. Reaching to late 30s, big room in a shabbypretty collective house, hustle, bedlife, shared-password Netflix, words, picking free herbs in the park, $100 car. All your queer sick friends on the internet, all the ones that slowly stump towards you, you to them. The blog posts you write on a level 6 pain day on a heating pad in your same fleece sleep pants you don't have the spoons to wash, space heater blasting, pain patches slapped on, that you post up and maybe someone sends you $20 in PayPal, someone thanks you, someone thinks it's bullshit.

Slow life, poor life, abundant in time and pain life, queercripfemmebrown writing life. Not the only one. Invisible to those who can't conceive of it. But here. Here.

Femme houses

1. This perfect pink house in South Central, your inheritance.
I see your room of your own, your bed, bong and books
Full pantry for now, cosmetics carefully curated:
I see the rich.
We smoke medicine and sleep well. You get up at four thirty
to drive me to the airport, ten minutes on the streets.
I runlimp to plane, don't want to release my arms from your disabled
    parking spot hug.
I see your femme abundance,
your row of grandmother's pompadour pictures from East Los in the '30s
your laugh crackle breaking out, how you say, *m'ija, take anything you
    need*.
This is your wealth.
You're here because your grandfather built this house,
left it to you. You will live here, building wordhouses,
femmehouses of your body, 'til you die. Maybe.

2. Home doesn't have to be forever to be home
I have it tattooed on my chest but I still forget,
daily. We've all lost our beloved places
to five dollar lattes and shiny white couples pushing children.
I want there to be neighborhoods they're afraid to go to.
I want them to know there are places they don't belong.
I want them to hate us, to fear us,
to not see anything pretty in our houses that makes them want to buy them
    up for cheap.

3. Once, I lived in a house for $175
for
fig tree and black mold and chill to the bone
and oven for heat
and it was ok to cry in front of the washerdryer,
it was ok to borrow someone else's fucked up car.
You could live off the eggs and kimchi in the pantry if you needed to.
We were always ready for the end of the world:
earthquake water   bags of grain.

We are always getting ready for the end of the world
and she keeps creeping. I thought a soft collapse and
I would live and die in that house.
Instead, whiteness refinanced its mortgage and moved back in.
Instead, I moved into more falling apart,
less pretty. Instead, I left the country again,
with two big bags on a plane and all my stuff on Amtrak.
Instead, I came back and squatted in
another neighborhood invaded by white. As soon as the laundromat lady
   knew me
to chinnod, I was on another plane
to a place I hoped would have water, and a house,
and it did, but it had cold and no sun.
We made a femmehouse. I wondered if my hipbones could relax.
They sort of did. Not like before.
I lost my child's trust in a here safe forever
I trust it is safe enough, now.

4. Their house has a pink canopy, a shower chair,
no stairs. Takeout burgers and makeup. Mess.

My house has a plum couch, a scrubbed tub, a hot tub. One stair.
Her house has an apothecary, flogger shouts,
a witch stoop. Her house has two cats, steak and weed in the freezer.
Their house has a crystal cunt,
rolling tobacco pouch, mama's picture.
We float in clouds and walk on earth.

for Meliza, Neve, Jesse Manuel, Sabina, Naima and me

I know crips live here

I know crips live here. So many couches and blanket throws.

I know crips live here. A bathroom filled with coconut oil, unscented conditioner and black soap.

I know crips live here. Your Humira and T on the bottom shelf of the fridge.

I know crips live here. Only house on the block with a homemade ramp, property standards are so mad.

I know crips live here. Big exhale at the shower chair, the slip pads and the air purifier.

I know crips live here. I see all the things in reach around your mattress of glory.

I know crips live here. Straws and Poise pads and crosswords and weighted blankets and stim toys.

I know crips live here. You've been home for a couple days. A week. That's the imprint of your ass in the couch surrounded by empty bags of food and the Advil and the heating pad.

I know crips live here. 50-pound bag of epsom salts from the farm store, your painkiller display like an altar.

I know crips live here. I see your EBT card and your fought-for DSHS care attendant.

I know crips live here. Taught yourself to be an herbalist so you could afford to manage your pain.

I know crips live here. Everybody late.

I know crips live here. Your dogs, cats and stuffed animals are part of your family.

I know crips live here. Your disabled parking placard a candle in the window.

I know crips live here.

Welcome
You are home.

(Inspired by Eli Clare's "Interdependence," in Brilliant Imperfection*)*

Bad road

"my body is 40 miles of bad road" —working class disabled saying

oh I know,
you mean well

but
when I say I hurt   when I say some part of
my body hurts   and you say, *oh, did you do something?*

I hear   *what did you do?*   As in, it's your fault,
there's cause and effect and there's a simple
there's a story, and if a + b = c, we can fix it

But there's no simple story in this body.
She falls apart whenever she feels like it,
which is often. She doesn't feel like going to
work or up and down three flights of stairs, and she'll tell you all about it.
She can smell the weather.
She got a lot of stories
and just like her mama did at slam church two decades ago,
she spits them out my kneecap like a gun with chaotic
yet accurate aim.
She is forty miles of perfect bad road
all bumps and potholes that could take out your wheel.
You gotta know how to drive it.
You gotta not be too worried about breaking your car
(because she's already broke   too)
I mean, I could tell you, everything happened! I could tell you my mama

molested me, I could tell you hers did too,
I could tell you we had to walk a long long way and get on a boat,
I could tell you I moved to Brooklyn for love, but there's a lot of stairs here
    too
I could read you the particulate matter of the air, that they're spraying for
    pesticides today
that I ran out of the fish oil that greases my knee into smoothing,
and I don't know if the CVS sells it here
—but does anyone want to hear all that?
The staying chant
the recitation
of everything that's happening in my body, and their body,
and the park's body, and on the subway huffing diesel and cigarettes

When you say, it's just pain for no reason all the time, fibro, right?
I say, close but no cigar!
I say I intimate with pain tides
This ground not steady! Why would it be?
As soon as I figure it out she flips me the bird
shape-shift hip transforms and says, *fuck you, you figure it out*
Sometimes the place where my mama threw me into the wall
at three talks to me and locks all my earth into cement.
Some days I don't know what day it is.
Some days my ass leaks tidal marsh, briny river
Some times everything   everything
everything   every thing
hurts
like a church bell
like a call to prayer
and it calls me to pray

this pain
breathing into any place that doesn't hurt
some of which only exists in my revolutionary imagination.
Sometimes you have to talk quiet.
Sometimes I can't talk at all.

Of course you don't believe that, but I feel the need to declare:
my life is worth living anyway
I love every jounce on this bad, bad
underfunded budget cut frost heave road
not everyone's car can make it down;
   you gotta know
   how to drive it
I love every car that just gave up in the mountain pass
every hubcap that fell off
every—yes—road not on any map
every rock and resisting
every reason this happened
every reason this body
is reason enough
for being.

Bed days

What were my mom's pain days like? Were they all of them?
She didn't have weed, friends, a therapist, yoga,
baths, Vicodin, T-3s, community acupuncture, fragrance-free or turmeric.
She had wine, silence and a garden. She had hidden.

Sometimes I lie in bed on a pain day with my sick and disabled friends
a finger swipe away, my twin canes,
my partner who loves me
my good bed, my nettles and my deep breaths,
and still the pain in my knees and legs lives and shouts fire, and I wonder

if my disability is me feeling all the pain
my mom never had a chance to feel
finally safe enough to come home and talk to me.

Crip magic spells

Beautiful baby crip, I come to you in your dreams.
There is so much nobody's going to tell you   for a while.
Please don't die. I promise something else is waiting and worth it.
You will know the names: *freak, inspiration, pain in the ass*.
No one is telling you
that disability is magic,
that crips are magicians,
that it is so very important that you live.

But we are waiting for you, this army of disabled family
no doctor or family member will tell you exists.
They will tell you the best you can hope for is being just like them
but we are waiting for you,
and we will be what will save your life.

We're here to tell you how we did it,
how we keep doing it.
We flourish the swords and wands of this artful way to live.
I am here to tell you that we know some of the best magic anyone knows.
We have already survived the worst things in the world
and we have so much joy and science the boring normals have no idea how
   to be
We are some of the best hot magic, the best best magic
we are the best   we are the best
we are the best best
the best   the best

Darling, let me show you your first magic trick.
Asking for help is the first and last spell you'll ever have to learn
It's the one everything else rests on.
It's the simplest, hardest thing.
You're going to ask for a chair
when you need one
You're going
to ask for the lights to get turned down
before you have the migraine.
You're going
to ask someone to not wear the perfume that kills you.
You're going
to ask.

I know you're already staring at me in disbelief
You've got those words
burden, whiner, don't ask them for too much
echoing in your skull
but
humor me.
Practice.
Practice.

Asking is femme magic
crip magic
submissive magic
Break your legs open to the world, girl!
Be in your power asking for just what you need.
Know that everyone deserves to get exactly what we need
There is no such thing as not disabled enough

There is no such thing as too disabled for this world.
Just because there's three months when you're not in pain
doesn't make your pain less than chronic
Just because you're in a chair doesn't mean you're in pain.

If we were really, *really* never meant to survive   Audre
what does it mean to insist
that if we're going to live, it will be glorious.
That we will have a wonderful youth
an ecstatic middle age
an orgasmic crone hood.
That we will get to live to be old.

It's the smallesthugest thing
you'll ever learn:
don't touch me on my back
I know I said it was ok before
but it's not now.
Bring me that dish
no, that one,
Every day is a new chance
to perfect your magic

All the femmes come back

Every time you die, I shout, *take it back*. I shout, *no*.

I think: it's not the real story. It's a mistake. You're going to come walking around the corner any minute. I'm gonna read your cards. We're going to hug, we're going to kiss, I'm going to have lunch with you. We're going to collaborate.

Every time you die I numb   I shout like I punched in the gut
I don't need any more ancestors   I got plenty
I walk   I drink whiskey   I more gray hair
I survive   I don't
I think you're going to come walking around the corner.
My lover wants to die. I want to die. We don't.
This is a war. I think we're losing it.

I promised after Taueret died, I would go to the hospital or pills or the woods forever rather than die. I still promise. Never is a promise. I see you, you're just about to walk around the corner. I walk around the corner to you.

All the femmes come back
walk out of the grave in your best dress
Roll out a mess
and be loved.
All the femmes come back
to enough excellent alchemist mental health care by the best witches in the
    world
to months to just lie there and be held

No emotional labor. No bullshit. No heartbreak.
I promise.
To be loved with all and no makeup

All the femmes come back, and I wash away rape,
I wash away racism, I wash away femmephobia
we witch away transmisogyny, we witch away ableism
I wash away every *too much, crazy girl*
I wash away every *not enough, you fucked that up*
I wash away every single way our hearts were broken and broken and
    broken and broken
and we were resilient! and we were strong!
and we glittered, and we got back up,
and we thought no one would love us if we weren't perfect
and we were often exactly right about that statement

and I wash away
every single place
god and your mama
all those ex-lovers   all those frenemies
told you,
better off dead,
better off dead than being in pain where somebody else can see.

Here are all the reasons I have not died so far that I can remember:
I chose life because I liked to eat. I chose life because I would be goddamned
    if my parents won.
I chose life to spite them. I chose life because something reached for me,
and kept reaching. I chose life
because a diner breakfast was two dollars and ninety-nine cents in 1998

and I would get full, and walk the four miles home when I still could do that
and sleep the suicide off for a minute.
I chose life because library books about incest & all-night rape crisis
hotlines where I was a repeat caller
were the way I healed when every therapist's low end of the sliding scale
    was way too high.

And the truth is, I healed because I wasn't pretty
or on the internet or popular or loved,
because I couldn't and didn't look like I had it all or anything together,
so I had nothing to lose by being ugly, crazy, a snot-filled mess of pain.
and even though I was sure I was a fucked failure
I healed slow in a basement filled with cheap meals
while no one was watching
but god. I was a wondrous mushroom.
I chose life as spiteful revenge and that
has held me when everything else
let go.

All the femmes come back
all the femmes no more ancestor
all the femmes this juicy fucked-up plum of now
all the femmes we make a place for you to stay
all the femmes
come back
come back
come back

Dedicated with love and rage to Jerika Bolen, Taueret Davis, Amanda
Arkansassy Harris, Bryn Kelly and Basil Arbogast
and all femmes in struggle with suicidality, including me

Adaptive device

I want to give you a poem like an adaptive device
that will hold you just as good
as your favorite cane   bed sling   accessible toilet seat
rescue ventilator   cigarette   crushed pocket Xanax
blanket weight   mad map sign.
Give you the words that are what I know how to do
Give you the words that will take meaning, make language
make a word house to hold you, open-doored and firm-roofed.
The steady tap tap thrum of your cane tip
The steady roll of the charged battery
of your chair, your brain, humming.

What does it mean to call a poem
an adaptive device? A piece of beautiful supportive tech
that puts in work to keep you alive?
Something your doctor will sneer at and never understand:
you mean you just walk around with a cane all the time?
Something the newly crip say
I don't want to be, you know, pathetic, I just need a little help.

This poem will never be found in a packet of home care instructions.
This poem is not taught in med school.
This poem is not behind the counter at the pharmacy or OTC.

If poetry is a means of telling the truth, June,
and poetry is as sturdy butterfly as the steady tap of my cane's dance,
then poetry is crip. Then truth is crip.
Then this poem be a crip hand to hold you.

This poem is short enough for even my memory to memory it!
This poem can be whispered or signed.
This poem unspools from a drooling lip
This poem can be tapped in and sung from augmented communication!
This poem spoken from gesture and nuance
This poem is nonverbal
This poem is crip kindness
This poem thinks you are desirable and love is coming
Is here. This poem will help you get on and off the subway.
This poem is a reason to live.

2. sacrum

Tonguebreaker: Taueret

1. My plane touches down at JFK. There's turbulence.
In the back of an Uber, I scroll Facebook, see *rest in power,*
powerful femme. I yell no to nobody.
Your friend tells me *she left us Saturday night, femme,*
like she said she would. I say, take it back. She says, *femme, I wish I could.*
I think,
that was you, making a big noise over Brooklyn,
rocking the plane's wings hard, all your fierce wind and lightning.
You always did what you said you would.
There really is no more you.

2. What would you have me do to mark your death?
Eat a big steak and drink good bourbon
Fuck well. All the decadent, beautiful
things you loved. You on the internet a week ago
selling all your gorgeous high-end sex toys you got from work:
how could no one have noticed?
How could I fuck with them?
How could I not?
What is the right way to memory you?

3. Who can out-stubborn you, stubbornest femme
cunty hippo bitch warrior?
The answer: no one.

4. I have gone as deep as you, I think. I can't know.
No one could out-cunt stubborn you,
including in your determination
to die.

5. *are they gonna play "Anaconda" at your funeral. did you leave a note.*
how is your mama gonna bury you. is she why you did it.

6. these deep Black femme waters. all you couldn't say. all the donated
banana pudding at your memorial. all the people crying. Surprised. I
wasn't surprised. You went out with a perfectly executed bang like the best
burlesque number you ever did.
You in that last instagram saying, *I just want to be a mess. Fall apart. Be*
   loved.

7. It wasn't just, *we should've loved you harder.*
It was more like, you needed this world to be better, to make you want to
   stay.

For Taueret Davis, March 28, 2015

Shark's mouth

My mom started raping me as a baby, and maybe that is why
I love a shark's mouth glittering with teeth
My cunt is a cracked-open geode
spilling with a million bladed gems.
A hole that grins, ripped open,
scarred from its opening and tearing,
still will cut you,
steel will bloom.
I would never have asked to be this other
than human, to carry this particular wound.
But this is the wound I carry. Born to? Unsure.
I bear my own self-defense, these glittering
broken blades, this innocent hungry smile.

Parliaments on the stoop

There's nothing like being two kinds of sore-hipped brown femmes
a week after a hate crime,
smoking Parliaments on the stoop
outside a queer Black femme birthday party
with lots of glitter house looks.
It's safe to be inside, soft,
but we come outside
to be bad brown femmes looking at the moon
smoking in the bushes like we've trained for at every wedding.
We're watching the Islamophobia meter go up,
tracing frequencies of hair pat downs and panic attacks,
saying, *it feels just like after 9/11, girl,*
saying, *I think the government paid him to do that shit, he ain't ISIL.*
He's probably some closeted gay cousin whose an asshole to his wife
like we've known plenty of in our lifetimes.
The queer Muslim healing gathering was in the basement of an inaccessible
   bar,
we left after five minutes.
Bad brown girls always cluster in a bush
sucking fire and blowing smoke at the moon,
at what we never know how to survive
but somehow, sometimes, do

For Fatima, after Orlando

This one broke my tongue

I started talking early
Mama! Like a shout and a snarl.
I taught myself
to read at two. I
followed the rope ladder
of words hand over hand
written and out and yet
my brain sometimes is still caught in a
steel trap.

My tongue thick, I can see the pictures,
I can't say the names.
I am the fastest slowest girl
Been yelled at for this all my life,
whatsamatterwithyou

I write with all my Aries lightning
to seed the way from the inside to the meaning
Text is my first language

I make my living from words
I am an amazing liar
I can talk my way into crossing the border and free beds from IKEA, I lie
all the time except in poetry and my everyday
word is bond.
I've always had a code, a secret language
a way words come down like a rope ladder
lowered from a sinking ship to a lifeboat

Text is my first language
Colors, sky, cloud, the fact of being:
the sacred prequel.

For Autistic Queer and Trans People of Color

suicide contract

i had to suicide contract w/ 3 people last week/
this week is better/ I haven't had to do that in 3 days

got *hard to kill* tattooed on my wrist
so it'll look fucked up if I cut
and cause it's true

died already
went down to the river
sucked a mouth full of mud
came up gasping

it's hard to be
the one who's good
at suicide

I'm on this shore
I can breathe under water
I can dive into that mud and

drag
all   of them
back
up

I don't fear death
and I do
I scream at her
I know her good

I was demon enough to live
not demon like she said
so be scared of me, mama
you'd best be scared of me

We are the ones
who survived
the abusive mommies and daddies
I'm what's left
after she was through

and

I
          got
a lot
left

my world
already ended and

I lived
I lived

demons are prettier
than they told you

Tonguebreaker

Sri Lankans have very long names
that break anyone else's mouth in half.
They give up two syllables in   They don't even try
They stammer. They make a bad joke
that we're used to

Central Mass femmes talk louder and faster than anyone else,
because when no one is listening to you, you just turn up the volume.
fuck you, white lady from Lexington,
two booths over glaring at me   you're going to hear what I have to say
whether you want to or not.

My name takes up all the room it wants
Yours should, too.
If they take our countries, our long-ass names
will insist on every syllable being pronounced
And if our names break the tongues of the unknowing and uncaring,
those who thought they knew our lands
and lied   well
that is the point.

Be as big and unapologetic as your fat femme ass spreading out on a bench.
I claim the right to be just as big and untranslatable
as every uncle with three initials and three names
that are each five syllables long

This world breaks us. This world breaks and breaks and breaks.
This world takes. This world will pile on one more thing after the last thing

you thought you couldn't stand.
You stand and sit. Serve tea until there is no more tea left in the world.
No matter. I keep my name. I keep my speed. I break your tongue.

3. bed life

microaggression magic

I replaced you with really good
winged eyeliner. I replaced you with short skirts
and breathing. I replaced you with the silence that lived
where you used to laugh at my hair.
I replaced you with *I don't want to hate/love/rage/*
fight no more

And what would it mean for me to love
with all my intelligence?

And what would it mean
to stop writing
those bitter, bitter
brokenhearted
femme of
color
love poems?

Note to Myself Six Months Ago, Or, Queer Brown Love Is a Magic Rainbow Fuck Unicorn Worth Waiting For

One day real soon, babygirl, you're going to have a brown femme lover
who, when they take you home to their dead grandma's house
in Elmhurst, Queens, on your third date,
you're gonna notice they have coconut, argan, castor oil *and* shea butter on
    the dresser.
Plus a big thing of Mixed Chicks leave-in conditioner.
The 64 ounce   The beauty supply special.
They're going to be like, *baby, do you want me to rub coconut oil on your*
    ass?
You're gonna think back to your last white ex
who used to always be like, *god, your hair's so crazy in the morning!*
You're gonna think, *that will never happen again.*
You're gonna think, *this is justice.*
You're gonna say, *yes, baby*
oh yes.

boxcutter beloved

My love sleeps with a boxcutter by their head.
They salt and baking soda scrub
off all the bullshit of life as an act of war.
Tells me, *move your altar back*
in your room, you need protection. My bb butter tongues
ice cream pints from grocery outlet for days
Says, *I love you so hard and so soft.*
Says, *Femme, I see your work.* Says,
femme bottoms are alchemists
we take all that pain in and transform it. I say back,
marry me don't marry me fuck me in the ass!
My beloved worth the work
of staying and staying
and staying

My love says femme is a beautiful knife, warm in the hand.
My love sleeps with a boxcutter on the windowsill, machete under their
   bed
They used to put a knife under the bed to cut the pain of birth
Femme, I see our work.

Prayer ghazal for Orlando

The day the shooting happened I turned off my phone and fucked my lover
We cleaned house and fixed things
nothing and everything in my life
has prepared me to face very hard things with a very good person:
this the place where we pray.

Our cunts are a dance floor, our bodies
with their abundance of brave queer openings
where we pray
our blessed mouths hunger
where we turn the phone off to
face each other, pray

The litany of lineup, of all night, of body,
of chair dance, of cane dance, of wheelchair hump
of every time
someone might have shot up
Manhattan's or Funkasia
found their way to Unit 2 or Quilombo
no, we pray

I love my love very much, I love them in exactly
every way my parents never prepared me to love anyone
I love this queer love neither of them got to enjoy,
I love every thing I learned on prayer bead queer club lineups
drinking overpriced jameson and ginger, chatting in crip corner
every time I made ritual of dressing up and then driving home with a
    burger alone

satiated and thigh sore, every place I dressed and wound
to find my body, every place
a prayer.

abundance

It's not that I don't believe in abundance.
it's that this world is so often abundant in bullshit
It's that my memories are soaked
in both the queer radical past present future
and in memories of lovers who treated me wrong.

My memories are quantum. Show me where I did right,
did the best, loved my solo femme slipping out into the perfume of themself
and how I did not know I could ask, not divine
it into being, by accident, when no one was looking.

It's not that I don't believe in abundance
It's that my time and spoons are not.
Are rich when grown in crip soil
This soil.

It's not that I don't believe in abundance
but I know that you have not been given an abundance of trust and land
and neither have I.
I know that there is not an abundance of crip femme brown survivors
being loved well, with all the nutrients and time it takes
there is an abundance of us saying,
it's cool, of us saying,
don't worry about it
I'll see you later   it's been real
We leave, we write the letter later,
or never
we don't even ask

We make solitude and absence look sweeter   we are the sweetening and
   the bitter

The sweetening and the bitter,
the world is not abundant in either of us.
This crip love special, not off-the-rack
I cherish you
Aaliyah was right: One in a million/7 billion
Who would I be if I did not raise lions around this crip brown femme
   house?
Who would I be if I did not value the abundance of us?

4. rust will cut you

Walking pneumonia:
a working class sick femme prayer

Soak your chest in Vicks, girl.
Shoplift some oil of oregano.
Thyme in boiling water, put a saucer over the top.
It'll bring out that golden oil. Honey—
get that phlegm up.

Mucinex, yes—it's a wonder drug, it came from an herb.
from a country some of us come from
But mostly, rest. You can't do "just a little bit of work."
You can't "go on just a short plane ride."

A roasted onion and some mustard in a compress on your chest.
It's cheap. Hit the $15 community acupuncture clinic. They will tell you to
    rest.

There's a real risk of walking pneumonia. But you knew that.
We walk through pneumonia all the time. We walk and roll through every
    damn thing.
Yeah, I know it's connected to grief. There will be more.

Chest aching from the barking cough   mountain of pillows.
Chicken soup in the freezer   cedar tea from the corner tree:
I've been there. I can working class femme MacGyver my way through any
    sick and tired.
Make it to and through the airport with my inhaler, cane, Claritin,
    decongestants and yin chiao.
Then my body collapsed, insisted I rest.

Working class femme lungs spread like aching, congested butterflies, wings
   beating but slow
slathered with every home remedy but rest.

Executive Order 13769, January 27, 2017

I have been waiting my whole adult life
for someone to blockade Checkpoint 5
For witches to come and sage and salt this place
For workers to get paid union rates
to dismantle the Scantrons piece by piece
and biomediate their radiation with mushrooms.

How many gallons of terror sweat are soaked into these floors?
How many times has someone I loved been waved over for a "genital
    abnormality"
How many times has TSA groped my friends' wheelchairs, swabbed
    their prosthesis for cluster bombs?
How much energy have I spent that could have gone somewhere else
praying, armoring myself and trying to pass

Instead of terror levels red, orange and yellow
for what the government is afraid of
there should be terror levels to mark how scared we are of them.
Are there cops with machine guns at the international terminal today?
or did the TSA agent smile at me once?

But here you are
The improbable future
A million emergent butterflies getting on public transit and heading to
    the airport
Not to fly
But to stay

For the Muslim ban airport protestors, winter 2017

The stories you tell to save your life

The thing about the stories you tell to save your life
is that you'll believe them:

I was a tough girl, a scary girl, a hawk a loogie in the gutter
and stomp away with five-inch platforms girl,
so I couldn't use my cane for years, or say when I needed to lie down

I was tough, no one fucked with me, I walked with a femmeswagger,
femmedagger,
so I couldn't admit when a girl was killing me with her eyes and hands

People thought I was that angry one because I was brown and femme and
    pissed,
had left my parents. They never saw the grief
because I didn't

When I fled my family what I knew was fierce relief and joy
They would never hurt me again, there would never be another
    screamed-at christmas
I would never hit myself to make what didn't show up in X-rays real.

I made love to my first apartments, shitboxes
with bad carpet and windows so moldy the frame fell apart in my hand
like someone else would polish wedding present crystal.
My solitude was my long joyful wedding with myself.

It wasn't until she started to die and I knew because I couldn't stop
crying, my head a grief migraine lightning strike

that I finally whispered, *I miss having a mom.*
I felt the terror they would show up and break up my wedding

Gratitude was a fierce dive in my chest telling my kid she was safe, she was
   safe.
I was her imaginary friend grown up whispering all the ways we made it
as I rocked arms wrapped around knees in my very own car.

I cried for months and then anger finally came to visit
My rage was perfect shellac red nail tips pierced with diamond dermals.
I was finally not so goddamn understanding.
I was finally furious at what they had both done.

Maybe because I had become their age and I knew they were adults
Maybe because if I could fight to find therapy for $20 they could've tried
   that too
Maybe because the gift of queerness is nothing is as it has to be

Maybe the gift of being a storyteller is I can keep rewriting my story.

Lightskinned for beginners

1. Calm the fuck down. You don't have to be all whisperscreaming, "I know I have white passing privilege, so I'm just so grateful you let me be here!!!!!!" at the go-round at POC yoga. It's ok. You can just say you're glad to be here. You are.

2. Everyone knows what you look like (except do they) (except the container changes how they see) (like the slope of a cornea shifting) (the container is always changing and so is the vision) (there is no one way to see, there are a million ways take in information without vision) (this is a disabled knowledge) (like the words folks know how to use) (like how they know how to see) (sometimes you get lighter with age) (sometimes you get darker when you move away from the PNW to someplace with sun) (in T'karonto or Queens you are just another brown curly hair light brown skin hazel-eyed one) (when you go home you are another lightskinned Tamil, privileged and normal) (they've seen you before) (whites and us, both) (they/we know you) (when they/we don't know you sometimes it's privilege and sometimes it's killing) and it won't kill you to acknowledge it (yes it's complicated) (you don't have to apologize, though) (apology for existing is not the same thing as accountability for the weird-ass common places we inhabit) (you didn't cause colonial rape or your parents or the weirdness of genetics) It will take you a while to figure this out (like every day (like the rest of your life))

3. Many Sri Lankans don't trip when they meet me because they've met some version of me before—there's a mad range of skin tones on the island and I look like some cousin they've seen at some point. However, I don't LOSE MY ENTIRE COMPLEX LIMINAL-ASS IDENTITY if I acknowledge that INDEED IT IS POSSIBLE SOMEONE MIGHT HAVE THOUGHT ONCE OR TWICE I WAS A WHITE JEW, PORTUGUESE OR A LIGHTSKINNED PUERTO RICAN AND, IN ANY CASE, NOT SRI LANKAN.

4. *passing* is different than *being read as*   the first is *you want to be them*, the second is *someone is seeing you as what you despise.* you are not trying to be the enemy, they are not your goal or your love.

5. Your dark-skinned and non-mixed-with-white friends don't always want to hear it. "it" being the weird moments of being in the airport or the grocery line when the gaze shifts: which are you, terrorist or nice girl? being asked what you are for the millionth time, having some white girl in the workshop say, *well, there's no people of color here.* They are Black or brown all the time. That is a different life, they might not want to hear about how badly you want it.

6. Of course, you can maybe be passing for/read as and then at any moment it falls to shit and then you're just another spic/towelhead/n-word/prairie n-word and your life is in danger. The enemy so angry they mistook which end of the blurring line you are on, that you are the product of someone (they think) fucking someone who shouldn't have been fucked, they want to beat you to death for it.

7. Knowing how to hang and crack a joke will go a lot further than constantly having a nervous breakdown. Shoplift the spray paint, don't shame spiral.

8. Don't date dark-skinned people to get cred or inject their genomes into your future baby. You think you're fixing history, but you might be making more scars.

9. Dating white people will also not always be a solution. You definitely will be the POC in the couple. Except for the times they will "forget"—all of them; they want it both ways and will get neither. Maybe they do love you. How do they know to love you. Maybe they will. Maybe it'll probably be tragic. It might be impossible to write about without playing into every love-sees-no-color scene you don't believe in.

10. The white parent who ironed your hair 'til it sizzled blood or how it was growing up with racists who are related to you. How if you are in a multigenerational lightskinned family, some or all of your family might be color-struck assholes, killers who have killed y/our own: Tell the story.

11. Tell the whole story. Resist the urge to write a heroic mango narrative of your ancestors. You were Sri Lankan at 8 in Worcester, MA, peeling paint off a falling-apart colonial garage. In the three photographs and hungry memories you hoard.

12. look for the role model lightskins who came before us, fought on the right side of history. the Jean Arasanayagams and Kathleen Cleavers, the Cherríe Moraga and Joanne Arnotts, the dudes who robbed the bank in *The Spook Who Sat by the Door* and Miklo Vargas becoming the head of La Honda in *Blood In, Blood Out*. the ones who did not love their white mom at the expense of loving themselves.

13. what legacy do you want to leave. what ancestor are you becoming.

14. when/if you live in a majority Black or brown city or country, the reference point bends away from whiteness and you might be not so damn white passing after all.

14a. change the frame, the stakes, the mirror. Ater the eye. You your own people your reference point.
Toi Derricotte said, *as I age, my face does look different, as if the bones of my Blackness have risen up to the surface*

15. So: surface yourself.

Small spaces

When I think of where home is, it's Ambal Trading at 591 Parliament St.,
    Toronto
The uncle at the front counter never looks at me like I'm a slut
I'm not his daughter, but I am family
There's a Tamil girl with blonde streaks digging in the fridge for curry leaf
    who smiles at me

Every time I'm in the rice aisle I stop
because I want to take home a 25-pound bag of red rice big enough to hug
but my suitcase is already full of 25 pounds of skirts, pills, epsom salts,
    backup shoes and sacred rocks
so I settle for two small bags of rice,
plus the best tea they have, a bag of jaggery, a jar of Maldive fish.
We have practice packing home into suitcases
and I am no exception

When I was a kid, home came in the round container
of Larich's Jaffna curry my appamma would mail my dad from Melbourne.
My mother always warned me it was too hot for me to eat
My father didn't know how to cook, so it stayed on its shelf
but I would look at it longing
I would sneak it out and sniff it late at night
It smelled like a home I'd never had that was waiting for me

These four blocks are history.
The first place Sri Lankans came after the war.
They called the St. Jamestown projects Sanjaytown because there were so
    many Lankans

The Tamil Workers Centre got firebombed by the other Tamil center
   because they were gay

This is where that one bar is where all the uncles go to get their dicks
   sucked
This is the field where Tamil Somali Jamaican soccer happens every
   summer weekend
This is home. One block. One store. A sack of red rice. A glance.
A shipped spice.
Home is a small house.

birth day

On my 42nd, my friend calls on WhatsApp, she sings me happy birthday in
    ghetto Italian
I think is French, we laugh, we both half understand romance and languages.
She says, *when we were first getting to be friends,*
someone I knew said, that's going to be hard
Well, they were masculine. Well, it was ——.
They said, two femme survivors, won't that be a challenge?
I tell her that when I am friends with friends
not femme, not survivor, they're from a different planet I don't speak the
    language of
That all my friends are femme survivors and it's a gift going on twenty years

I used to think we were only cartoon hearts and lightning strike burn.
Now I see us as long winding river curving each other closer and farther
Maybe if it's hard to be friends with a femme survivor
it just means you're bad at being friends with us.
Maybe you think trauma only stays in the shape of brand,
not decoration, bridge, library, seed archive.
At 42 I make a beautiful dress of all my scars
Scar tissue is the strongest tissue in the body
Maybe you are unlucky if you do not have a card to its library.

Perhaps the ones making that statement
thinks femme only comes in the shape of pretty
I've always been far more interested in femme in the shape
of ugly and dangerous,
monstrous and ordinary.
I want to be monsters with my femmes

Our monster is how we lived through this.
I want us to monster large together.
a perfect knife, broken and studded,
I love us, born broken blade,
our love languages we half know celebrating each other's birth

5. ritual prayers: performance texts from mangos with chili

introduction:
qtpoc disabled ritual prayers

The following pieces are longer performance texts I wrote and performed with and for Mangos With Chili, the queer and trans people of color performance collective and tour I cofounded and codirected from 2006 to 2015—as in, almost a decade of wild adventures, hard learnings, mistakes, beauty and working class femmes of color making our dreams real. These pieces were created and performed in a very specific moment in time in the Bay Area of California, when QTPOC art and politics were blooming, when we could all still afford to live there.

In Mangos, we believed that performance was/is political. Our shows were rituals, healing spaces and places that created and sustained the community we wanted. We produced our performance spaces as a place to gather, dream and create/remake ourselves by telling stories. This looked like everything from La Chica Boom doing performance as her alter ego Chico Pow (the worst MECHistA fuckboy you could imagine), saying things like, "Gloria Anzaldúa? Yeah, I'll fucking do her!" while the audience vented their rage at brown misogyny by hurling tortillas at the stage (sweeping up all the tortillas at midnight with fibromyalgia was hell) to performers cutting their arms in blood offering for the ghost of Gwen Araujo to an invented Black Queer Church service, the Congregation of Liberation. We did a million brilliant things and made a million mistakes.

In the time we flourished in the Bay Area, from 2008 to 2015, we did three large annual shows a year. This was an evolution from our original conception of our performance project as a tour, a QTPOC version of other, white-led and majority white, queer performance tours popular at the time that excluded us. And while we did do five North American tours in our time, we became more focused on doing local Bay Area shows, especially after the 2008 economic collapse made financing our work challenging, and after many of our tours proved to be both amazing and completely exhausting and, as a friend says, 1,000% Bananatown.

There is so much I can say about the Bay Area Mangos shows—how we performed everywhere from long-standing BIPOC-controlled theater spaces like the African American Art & Culture Complex, La Peña, Brava Theater and EastSide Arts Alliance to an ever-changing roster of legendary QTPOC performance spaces that gentrification shut down, like Mama Calizo's Voice Factory, The Lab and The Living Room Project. Our shows were fueled by little money, 20 to 40 volunteers, a very intent fan base, a muscling of internet 2.0 (like searching for "QTPOC and (name of city)" and cold-calling tiny social groups in cities we were visiting, saying, "Hi, you don't know me, but I codirect this QTPOC performance tour and we're coming to town, can you tell all your friends?") and thousands of hours of unpaid labor. As a co-coordinator, I often worked 'til 2 a.m. six days a week. The mixtapes we played as folks entered and the community altars we built were just as much a part of the show as our 3-hour-long, meticulously crafted performances that invariably started 40 minutes late. Love and sex and death and ancestors and hot dates and sold-out tickets and beauty and see you at the show.

Our performances were part of a rich culture of QTPOC performance art in the Bay in the 2010s, where we were one of many collectives, from Stories of Queer Diaspora to Queer Rebels to Peacock Rebellion to Topsy-Turvy to Culture Fuck, wrapped up in a web of collective houses, dance parties, play parties, protests, attempts at land projects, healing justice, disability justice and crafting, art and music spaces, organizing against gentrification, anti-Black racism, for Indigenous rights and immigrant rights. Drama and love, pain and healing, community and coldness and trying to survive under capitalism. I am forever grateful for the work we did, to have spent my 30s learning, growing, loving, being wounded and fucking up and winning inside that space.

Doing Mangos was work that was the love of my life. It was also incredibly exhausting in ways I didn't let myself feel until it stopped happening. It was also a place where, when I started out, I wasn't out about being disabled or Seriously Mentally Interesting or autistic. In the time I did Mangos, I would start performing with Sins Invalid, have my world rocked by disability justice and what it insisted was possible to ask for and do as a disabled performer, change what I thought I was allowed to ask for and how out I could be as disabled.

The pieces in this section are pieces that were created for Mangos shows—pieces on love, desirability and, increasingly, pieces where I dipped my toe in what it could mean to bring QTPOC pieces about disability to nondisabled-specific QTPOC spaces. Most of them were conversations with specific queer of color literary ancestors about chronic illness, legacy/role modeling and memory. Mangos emerged out of mourning and rage at how too many second-wave queer of color writers and artists—Gloria Anzaldúa, Marlon Riggs, June Jordan, Barbara Christian, Sylvia Rivera, Marsha P. Johnson, Barbara Cameron, Audre Lorde, Essex Hemphill, Assotto Saint—had died in their 40s and 50s in the 1990s and 2000s. We wanted to fill the gaps their deaths and the deaths of institutions they created like Kitchen Table: Women of Color Press had left. We saw our work as emerging from the lineage of QTPOC ancestors, of facing and surviving death. It makes sense that most of my pieces were in this vein. As a disabled person who has lived close to death, it also made sense.

What I had called myself had evolved—always poet, but from slam/spoken word poet to writer/poet to, in the time of Mangos, performance artist. As I grew as a writer, around 2005 I started to wonder about what ways existed for me to tell a story that was bigger than what a 10-minute poetry set could tell. I was curious about storytelling, the stage, ritual space, and was part of a cadre of performers experimenting with the same, and learning from more seasoned performers like sharon bridgforth who had been merging ritual and performance for a while. Mangos became a place where I got inspired by other QTPOC artists to do bigger and bigger pieces to serve the community. We worked on these shows for months, for hundreds of hours—directing, producing, promoting, fundraising and performing in—plus, in access years, doing all the access support—all of this work: for shows that ran for one or two nights only, max. We videotaped them and, later on, livestreamed them. But there were performances that existed in finite moments in time. You had to be there. The performance rituals weren't just the text, they were the stance, the breath, the ritual objects, the crowd in its fancy outfits, flirtation and creation of a temporary community.

Two years after our last show, I had almost forgotten about these pieces. But soaking out a spinal arthritis flare pain in the tub on the last day of Memorial Day weekend, I remembered them. I want to archive them here. Transcribing them makes me think about what my teacher the great Black Arts Movement poet Sekou Sundiata once said: "The page poem is the musical score, the performance of the poem is the melody." We come from Black and brown traditions like the griot, the storyteller, or Sri Lankan traditions of ritual theater and dance using puppetry, live acting, dance and music. And we as performers are only one part of the performance—those who witness, perceive and create a temporary community space to take in performance are the rest. But I offer these words as transcripts of moments in time of ritual healing that can travel and be remembered.

The texts that follow include notes about movement and staging, and also some notes about where and when the show happened and some of the story of the making of it.

daughter of kali and oshun

Written and performed for *Mangos With Chili Presents: Whipped: qtpoc stories of love, desire and disaster*, mama calizo's voice factory and la peña, sf and berkeley, ca, february 2009.

Show notes: *This performance was staged with a loop of images playing behind me as I read the words—a collage of images of love goddesses from South Asian and West African communities, self-portraits (early, pre–cell phone selfies taken with a digital camera), pictures of femme of color friends, ancestors and role models, pictures of myself and lovers, pictures stolen from the internet of high school classmates in traditional marriages, images of QTPOC couples, chosen family and dream homes. Basically, a collage of images of imaginary love and home. This piece came together when I was right at the beginning of what would be a looooong process of beginning to unpack the ways I thought of myself as ugly and undesirable, and to, as I approached 40, examine what a happy life would mean if I was rejecting mainstream and homonormative ideas of what "adulthood" looked like (marriage, kids, homeownership) and what femme middle age hood and elder hood would look like. I can't believe I wrote this almost 10 years ago. I had a lot to learn, mostly, of course, the hard way.*

Staging notes: *Stage dark. Images come up. Lights come up on Leah, stage right front, she stands in front of a mic stand and a music stand.*

happy valentine's day, everybody!
33. single. glowing. mostly happy.

I have lists, requirements, figures for the lovers I pick out.
not before their Saturn return. not before therapy.

I am fine. with or without
but there's a place on the back of my neck I can't kiss by myself.

dear lakshmi
dear oshun,

it's me again!
what bitches you are!
oh wait, are you going to jinx me for saying that?
oh momi, I may have had an image of you on my altar for a long, long time
but that doesn't make you any easier to figure out.

what is femme adulthood?
is it twenty pretty slips?
a pretty boy on my arm?
a full-time job and a mortgage just like mama but with pussy?
where are my femme elders?
the ones I need to show me how to do this? how to get older as a femme
be no longer girl, be what's somewhere between girl and elder that thing I
    guess is called adult
are they dead? disappeared? so many things try to kill us femme girls of
    color
do my elders know how to do this either?

lakshmi, oshun, I've prayed to you and bitched to you like all of us do.
Gotten down on my knees and wailed for a new lover, some sugar honey,
a daddy, someone's knees in my ass in the middle of the night, their arm
around my belly, holding me here.

I look at the facebook pictures of kids I went to private school with, me on
scholarship, them not at the husbands,
houses and babies they've chosen, that make them content.
make them think: this is it, adulthood, I've arrived. I am happy. I can coast.
or the queer friends I know, including some who used to be my youth,
who chose couples, partners. marriage the way we do it.
something beautiful with promise and certainty. that body next to us in the
bed. that conversation that will go on and on and on for years.
don't we all want something to hold on to?

I chose something different. single at 33, I feel the wind rushing between
my thighs and it's both freedom and fear. who will hold me, keep me safe?
will I still be beautiful and valued if I don't have a pretty butch on my arm
like a rock? my mother was married a year at my age, and that was late in
the '70s. miserable, but she still held on to her man, her house, her misery,
her solidity.

what is femme adulthood?
what will keep me safe?
make sure I'm loved enough?
what do I have if I don't have a man, a butch or a marriage?

I have twenty vintage slips in my closet,
19 books with my name on them
all those work accomplishments
a room of my own.
¾s of a master's degree. I have my skin. my independence. my ability to
know joy in this body. the knowledge no one will ever hurt me. I
have girls who love me.
all the lovers whose pillows I've left honey dust behind on.

I have love
I have love
I have love

as much as I miss the way she makes me feel, the promise of that daddiness
    filling the hole
the sweet spot on the back of her neck being everything, I have held on to
the knowledge that the only safety is in holding on to how it all changes.
right when I think I know how it's gonna go, diosa, you pull the rug right
out from under me! been bottoming to orisha and you all my life. that's just
how it is

what is femme adulthood?
what is enough?

when my beautiful friend went to a totally nice brown queer girl house
party filled with couples with mortgages and two jobs to pay for them and
furniture—I mean, real furniture—and she sunk in her chair on DayQuil
drinking a lot of wine, she said, I was like, is that what adulthood was like?

I didn't know. but I asked her what she would want instead

and she said, I would wish that I would wake up in a little house every inch
of which I knew was mine, filled with trinkets from all my journeys, each
one full of memory. I would rise and walk through my house wrapping
silk around my body, knowing that everything here was mine, and every
moment of every day of my life I got to choose exactly what I wanted to do.

our grown-up femme lives are the gifts unwrapped we promised ourselves
    as children

as we make new families that are something beyond couple
femme families that hold us
families that hold us so much more than our birth families did
we make up our own answer to the questions that plague us
and are held in all the ways we desire

write ourselves into history
just like has been done before
and how it's never been done before
but how we always dreamed it could be
wrapped up like a present we promised ourselves when we were children

(lights out)

the amethyst room

Created for *Mangos With Chili: Reclaiming the Rites: performance honoring the sacred of our queer and trans of color lives*, African American Art & Culture Complex, San Francisco, CA, National Queer Arts Festival, June 14, 2012.

Show notes: In Reclaiming the Rites, *we asked eight performers and six video artists to create work on different QTPOC rites of passage—birth, leaving home, violence, queer love and heartbreak, chronic illness, healing. I advocated for and chose "the rites of chronic illness." This show was one of the first shows Cherry and I produced together after an almost* two-year-long *conflict that was incredibly painful and that we didn't speak of to almost anyone for fear of losing our grant money. Creating this work was the first time I had created work on chronic illness and disability for a QTPOC audience that was not specifically focused on disability. Doing so was a risk and a big challenge, but it also was incredibly rewarding to bring work about disability to QTPOC folks who might be hesitant about attending an all-disabled show. This is a piece I loved, which I also brought to our 2013 Toronto and Ontario tour. I've retired it because it involved scattering dirt in a circle on the stage, as a metaphor for the "dirty laundry" of talking about disability—and, as it turns out, nobody likes to sweep up or dance on dirt immediately after your piece.*

Staging notes: Room is dimly it. All the text below is prerecorded as a voice-over, which plays as Leah moves around stage. There is a cot center stage back. Leah is lying on it as lights dim up. There are a small collection of family photographs and a candle clustered together at the east, to stage left. There are diyas at stage front center and a bucket of compost or dirt at stage right.

Voice-over text:
If chronic illness and disability have ritual
this bed is my altar
the place I circle and return to
the place I rest
the place I am dismembered
and am reborn
over and over again
the place where I live when I am too sick to go out
and the place where I make my own dance party

Movement notes: Leah rises slowly, using the physical language of someone rising from sleep who is in pain. Leah picks up bundle of herbs to front of cot and walks slowly to the family photographs to the east.

if prayer is repetition
and intention
and change

if chronic illness is the bed
here is where i pray

Leah faces east and kneels, holds bundle of herbs aloft without lighting it.

east: the ones who came before

ancestors who survived so much
whose trauma and life lives in my bones
who are the reasons my bones ache

let me honor you in my body
by listening to and living in this ache
(lights candle)
let me know that my pain is you reaching for me

Leah walks slowly from the eastern altar to the southern altar, which is at stage center front. When Leah gets there, she kneels as voice-over continues.

1993, 1995, 1997, 1999

surviving abuse bleeds into chronic illness bleeds into depression. I don't know when I got sick. When did I first need to sleep 17 hours a day and awoke still unable to find words, go to the bathroom, finish a sentence? when did my legs give out? when was walking to the bathroom an epic journey?

My entire adult life has been marked by illness. It's hard for me to tell when the pain, butterfly balance, fatigue and immune transparency I name as fibromyalgia really started. A childhood filled with abuse, and a need to sleep as much as possible, bleeds into a chronically exhausted yet over-achieving college years, scholarship girl on the 17 meetings a week plan. bleeds into the early 20s when I walked back into my incest memories, got sick and spent a lot of time on my futon.

fifteen years later, writing my memoir, I call those years the chronically ill years but i never called them that then. for me chronic illness was just life. you didn't add any more names to your list if you didn't have to.

south: kali/oya

100

whirlwind that knocks me on my ass over and over. i curse you and am in love with you. you are the tornado that knocks my house down, sends the asbestos flying, sucks out every toxic thing that needs to go. i hate how you knock down every bit of stability I scramble for. but your whirlwind transforms what needs to transform. you are the reason I am the one who changed everything in my family. **(lights candle)** let me sit with you. let me fall in love with you. let me never forget

Leah stands, picks up bag of compost, walks scattering dirt to the left and right. It should form a circle around the stage.

2000: I'm not sick anymore. Not like before. I don't tell my first good job, the job that is getting me barely out from under the poverty line. I think they will fire me if i say the word disability. i think they'll say you're not really disabled. I lean on them for part time, short hours, plentiful days off. I rest for so long after my four-hour shift

I don't want to live in a homeopathic stockade anymore. I want to be what i think a normal, a nondisabled 25-year-old is, so i start smoking again. I stay up 'til 4 a.m. every day of the weekend going to the club and the diner. I heal that way. I conceal how sick I am after with pack-a-day smoke, vodka liver and the fear of falling over. I know some other queer folks of color with chronic illness, but all we know how to say to each other is, *it sucks, right?* We don't know that this body can be anything more than shame. We don't know that our sick bodies have smarts that nondisabled bodies don't have. That they live in history.

2007: I move. Everything changes. I was so afraid to leave my free ontario health care. but there is California sunshine, community acupuncture for twenty bucks. There are also people who will carry my groceries up the stairs when my legs buckle. There's a cane. There is me, finally able to use it, finally able to ask for help because it is given without pity. I am able to do these things because there are crips who look like me, and different. Together, we begin to remake the world and my life is remade.

west: love

I name this bed, this altar, as the sweet, sweet, dark place of constant crossing transformation.

2012: we make love in bed. we make love. we do. every part of me wants to make a sarcastic joke about those words before, but what we do is make love. and that making love, sick crazy body to sick crazy body, that understands each other so well, that making love is part of the healing of the world.

we make love by napping. we make love by you bringing me a tray with skullcap tea, bananas, hummus and crackers and then cupping me, allowing me to slow down, to sleep.

our dates start at four in the afternoon because of course we will be tired by ten. of course we want to make love for at least six hours. you show me you love me by sharing your horde of ativan and pneumonia antibiotics. i show you i love you by showing up with two bags of fried chicken and strawberries when your asthma's turned to pneumonia in west oakland smog. we fuck between coughing bouts. between me yelling and flirting alternatively with the kaiser staff. you lean into me waiting on the meds line, i take your scent into my nostrils and breathed deep, felt your arms around my waist, my crooked hips, holding me up.

early on you brushed my cheek, murmured, i *want to experience the divine*
   with you

we did/in these bodies that understood each other so well, we did.

north: the body

if disability has rituals **(standing and walking to stage center, in front of
   the cot, facing audience)**
this body is my altar
the body is the daily practice
what I return to
over and over again
the only place I will ever own
I begin by listening

if our bodies are disabled divinity
this crip making love is part of the healing of the world

Lakshmi, you are a healer
You don't fix my body into a perfect able-bodied mold
you heal me by loving this one

Bow. Lights off.

a requiem for Gloria

created for *Beloved: A Requiem for Our Dead: because we refuse to forget you*, The Living Room Project, West Oakland, CA, November 3, 2012.

Show notes: *This performance was staged at The Living Room Project, a much-loved healing justice community space created by Black queer DJ and doula Micah Hobbes Frazier, at the legendary lofts at 1919 Market Street in Black West Oakland. The Living Room Project was Micah's home, a large loft space where parties, performances, meetings, healing justice spaces and workshops were held in the 3 ½ years it existed from 2011 to 2015. We chose TLR as the space for our 2012* Beloved *showing over conventional theater spaces because we wanted to support a Black queer community space. We also wanted a space that felt like a living room, like a home. Maybe also all the spaces we would've used were too expensive and booked. The show was one of our patented start-an-hour-late, three-hours-long masterpieces. We had to rent bleachers from SOMArts and get them driven to the space in a flatbed truck over the Bay Bridge. The show was filled with ghosts, longing, memory, packed bodies, offerings at the altar, tears and tech done last minute by the great Guatemalan femme poet and theater artist Maya Chinchilla—shit was so hectic we texted each other cues as the show unfolded.*

The show happened immediately after Hurricane Sandy had flooded much of Brooklyn and New York. Friends were organizing food battalions and walking up and down 12 flights of stairs to charge and recharge crip friends' vent batteries. In this moment of climate apocalypse fear and mutual aid, we hovered on the brink, looking fearfully at what we feared and knew was coming. Six years later, after a summer and fall of fires and floods, it's interesting to remember that pre-Trump, pre-apocalypse time.

The 1919 Market Street lofts were bought by a greedy developer and demolished in 2015, destroying the community that rooted there. The Living Room Project, like many Oakland QTBIPOC spaces, now lives in the aerial roots of our memories and imaginations.

Staging notes: There is a large 10-foot-by-10-foot projection of an image of Gloria Anzaldúa in midlife, in a button-up shirt and pants, standing in the shallows of the ocean, smiling, on a screen behind the performer. It takes up as much of the screen as possible and stays up throughout the performance. Leah stands before the projection, speaking into a microphone on a stand.

Leah: Kit Quan, one of Anzaldúa's oldest friends and writing comadres explains, "Gloria always told me that she was going to stick around for twenty more years. She struggled with diabetes and all its complications daily ... but she was so well read on the disease ... and worked so hard at managing her blood sugars that I believed we still had more time."

you can be the smartest crip in the world and still die.

dear gloria,

hey ma. how you doing?
dear gloria,

you died eight years ago today.

dear Gloria,

it's October, the day before Halloween. yesterday, a giant storm smashed into the Caribbean and all up the east coast. the photos of the subway looked like what I've spent my entire life thinking the end of the world would look like, my generation, growing up on rising waters, climate change, crumbling cities, everyone swarming for a generator and gas and dried food. my friends spend their days using facebook on phones to find gas and able-bodied people who can walk 12 stories of dark stairwell to take and replace exhausted batteries for our friend who is on the 12th floor with his ventilator. for the past month I have been waiting to find out if i have ovarian or uterine cancer or not, without health insurance. I stayed up last night 'til 2:30 in the morning clicking updates on my close friends feed, looking for updates about the nuclear power plants in Jersey, prisoners stuck on Rikers Island who were not evacuated, disabled people left in hospitals and nursing homes to die. I did this while I wrote the outline for an all-day disability training an organization wants to hire me to do. The power was out in Aurora's rehab facility, the food she can eat spoiled. A friend posted shots of Eric Drooker's graphic novel *Flood!*, where New York is completely submerged by water, saying, *we read that in bed in 1995.*

17 years ago this possibility teased us. now it's a reality, and I have sometimes a lot and sometimes little faith that we will all unite to take care of each other, survive to make something better.

Gloria, I want capitalism to be over already. I want the white capitalist colonialist ableist patriarchy to be over already. I want there to be guaranteed annual income for everyone, a little extra for those who are immune- and energy-compromised and can only work flexibly part time. I want guaranteed free personal care attendant service for everyone who is disabled, older, has kids or just needs it. I want health care that is free to everyone, I want a world where no one will ever have to raise money on the internet for an ultrasound, IV antibiotics or a new wheelchair to replace the one stolen by another desperate crip. Or, as I had to last week, argue with a medical receptionist who doesn't want to give me the transvaginal ultrasound ordered by the PA at the queer free clinic, who looks at me and Devi and says blankly, "It's $165 per body part, how many are you getting done?" and I wonder if she's counting the ovaries as one or two.

1979: Gloria Anzaldúa decides to devote life to writing, takes series of part-time lecturer and writer-in-residence jobs to buy as much time to write as possible.

1991: Gloria wins NEA grant, uses it to buy house in Santa Cruz by her beloved ocean, so she can visit daily.

A quote from Borderlands: *"It is dark and damp and has been raining all day. I love days like this. as I lie in bed I am able to dive inward. Perhaps today I will write from the deep core."*

Me too, ma. In these words, I feel your queer disabled woman of color artist hustle. I have worked so many hustles. *house cleaner tarot card reader shipping and receiving mini-mart cashier test subject landscaper phone sex operator telemarketer flyer girl small-time mover crisis hotline counselor, abortion counselor, rape crisis hotline supervisor, admin assistant, tenant hotline eviction counselor, writing teacher, anti-oppression workshop teacher performance artist gynecological teaching associate college lecturer guest lecturer bookstore clerk artistic collective codirector transcriber standardized patient journalist*

I have felt myself blessed. I have filled a savings account and emptied it whenever anyone needed rent. I have run up credit cards. I have run on debt and payed it off. I have been on income-based repayment for forever. I have passed a twenty-dollar bill back and forth across the movement. I have driven friends to the hospital and been driven to the hospital.

I have had to work part time and flexible and okay or salvageable when I get sick over and over again. I have done that and called myself lucky. I have traveled all over the country, had marvelous adventures, had lean times and hard times and better times and mostly been so glad that I have a life where i can afford coffee, value village shoes and time to write, where i can have marvelous adventures, where i can be part of changing the world.

I have been banking on the end of this world to happen so I would have a retirement fund, though.

Gloria, yesterday I taught the clinical breast exam to UCSF med students. it's $80 an hour for four hours total work time, an hour commute each way, half hour unpaid break. I brag about how hot shit I feel. I know how to teach the tits like whoa and if these stupid motherfuckers listen, they will learn how to detect breast cancer in their patients. I stood there and let these students feel me up medically, and i realized I would be getting a $340 check in a couple weeks, and once they graduated, they would be making $150,000 a year. I thought, *I should go to fucking medical school.*

And this is what I wonder as I look to you and your cohort of marvelous queer women of color poets who died in your 50s and 60s. I look to you more than I do to my biological family for answers. guideposts. life pathways. the miracles we make.

So what do we do, we queer people of color artists? do we have a full-time job and do this on the side? if we do that, do we get academic jobs, hang on by hook or by crook, doing essential war work but the micro- and macroaggressions build up and give us cancer and mental unhealth? Do we get an NEA and buy a house? does our lover take it when we break up 'cause it's in their name? do all our books go out of print like Chrystos? WHAT IS THE OTHER OPTION? I think about this shit all the time. I have faith in us. but, man, is it hard sometimes.

my friend said, *hey, we're the success stories! nobody ever told us it would mean we were still this broke.*

dear gloria: I listen for your echo. my life like so many stands in the outline of yours. there's that quote: the dead give up their bodies, the sick amongst us get practice, but i don't think that's exactly correct. i am living in the altered, everyday normal states of my body.

Queer disabled Puerto Rican/Jewish elder Aurora Levins Morales writes to you, "What I'm really interested in is that state you named after your ancestral goddess, the Coatlicue state, in which a shattering lets in light. Of course being Boricua not Mexica I call it the Guabancex and Oyá state, after the storm goddesses, the deities of creative destruction, of my Taíno and West African ancestors. The landscape of my homeland is regularly uprooted by hurricanes, those wild, whirling, spirals of wind and water spreading out vast arms to pluck trees and houses and lives from solid land, drive bits of metal right through tree trunks and take giant bites out of cement.

"In the structure of a hurricane, the strongest, deadliest winds are closest to the core, but the core itself is clear, calm, full of light. Illness has been one long hurricane season for me, chunks of cement and metal roofing flying through the air, big trees made into heaps of splinters and shredded roots. What takes me to the core, to the place of new insight is listening with all my being to the voice of my own flesh, which is often an unbearable task. What lets me bear it is political, is a deep, ecological sense of the web in which my flesh is caught, where the profound isolation of chronic illness forces me to extend my awareness beyond individual suffering ...

"In the steepest pitch, the darkest hour, in the ring of deadly wind, the only salvation is to expand, to embrace every revelation of my struggling cells, to resist the impulse to flee ... When my body feels as if it's tearing itself apart, when I'm in the nightmare condition, shaking and nauseated, my vision full of flashing lights, my legs too weak to stand, the only path out is deeper."

there is no place in the world to do what we do. except the secret places. the abandoned land. the mined places. our bodies in bed and on the line and sending texts about gas, writing poetry, supporting each other, sharing gas and food. and the world's unexpected changes. all we don't know and know yet. all that's happened that you've watched since you passed.

The only way out is deeper. The only way out is what we construct, together. Out of the bones of our best wildest dreams, our cripbrownfemme knowledge. Out of the arc of the bones of your life.

Always, mama. Thank you.

Love,
Leah

crossing the river jordan:
a lovesong for Marlon Riggs

Created for *FREE: Two Spirit, Queer and Trans People of Color Visions of Freedom*, National Queer Arts Festival, African American Arts & Culture Complex, San Francisco, CA, June 11, 2013.

Show notes: This was the last piece I created for a Mangos show. We had a wild idea that we would pair QTPOC artists to create new collaborative work—a vision that had mixed results because, as ever, we only had $200 to pay people. Because I was focused on directing, my performance was put together at the last minute. I had stumbled upon a short documentary on Marlon Riggs's life online while I was lying in bed being sick as per usual, and my mind was on Riggs as a Black queer HIV+ artist whose life and work embodied freedom. It made me think about how I had first encountered his work when he had just died and I was 20, with the great good fortune to be taking Gary Lemmons's Black Masculinities at the Margins class at Eugene Lang College. Professor Lemmons taught Essex Hemphill and Marlon Riggs, Joseph Bean and Assotto Saint, and many more queer Black feminist male writers and filmmakers. Many of the artists we studied died during the run of the course, or had died the year before we read their work. I was struck by the ways in which people remembering Riggs remembered his disability—negatively and positively, struggling with it—and the ways in which he made art as he got more and more disabled, directing from his hospital bed, speaking honestly about what it was like to be a Black queer filmmaker making films when he was close to death. In his practice as a disabled Black artist making work while sick, I found strength and a role model.

Staging notes: *This piece integrates clips from* I Shall Not Be Removed,[2] *a documentary film about the life and work of gay HIV+ Black filmmaker Marlon Riggs.*

The piece opens with the stage in darkness and a film clip of Marlon Riggs, ill, wearing a sweater, speaking to a packed auditorium at UC Berkeley, saying:

"And I was in the hospital for six months. Died nearly twice. There was one moment where I had such pain, such wrenching, catastrophic pain, I started to sob and roll back and forth. The nurses couldn't do anything for me. The doctors couldn't do anything for me. My grandmother, who stands next to me in all things, had to leave the room.
And my mother walked over. Took me into her arms like a baby. She said:
'Mommy knows
mommy knows
mommy knows
Sweet baby
Harriet's come to help you again
Harriet's here
Don't worry, baby
You've seen rivers like this
You've known pain like this
You stepped into the water
You've crossed
You've made it to the other side.'"

---

2. *I Shall Not Be Removed: The Life of Marlon Riggs*, directed by Karen Everett, screenplay by Barbara Christian (San Francisco, CA: California Newsreel, 1996).

(Image of giant river with feminine Black voice singing, "Precious lord, lead me on, let me stand."
Image freezes on river.)

Leah:

We all have crossed rivers
We are crossing rivers right now
If we're lucky, have people who help us cross it.

I saw Marlon Riggs's work for the first time in 1995, when I was twenty years old, almost twenty years ago. I was a lucky, lucky junior in college, taking a class called Black Masculinities at the Margins taught by Professor Gary Lemmons.

In that class, we read all kinds of queer Black men writing about all kinds of lifesavingly extraordinary things. We watched movies like *Looking for Langston* and *Young Soul Rebels*. We read Assotto Saint and Essex Hemphill's poetry. We read *Brother to Brother*, the first book of queer Black men's writing I'd ever seen.

And we saw Marlon Riggs's work. Marlon, this brilliant, brilliant queer Black snap diva genius artist. Marlon's film *Tongues Untied*, a poetic documentary of Black queer men loving Black gay men, aired on PBS in 1989. 1989, when Reagan was in the White House. Jesse Helms was banning queer artists from getting NEA grant money. 1989, where there were no queers on tv anywhere, Marlon, you shot a film where queer Black men made love to each other that I could watch on my television. Marlon, you said Black gay men loving Black gay men was the revolutionary act of the 1990s.

I was going to ACT UP meetings and giving out condoms to kids on the sidewalk because Giuliani had made it so you had to have parental permission to get sex ed in the middle of an AIDS pandemic that was murdering Black and brown people, queers and junkies. My first girlfriend's boyfriend before me had shot himself in the head at the kitchen table after his HIV results came back positive. And I wanted and needed, deeply, to learn how to love my queer colored self.

I still remember when Gary came into class on World AIDS Day, December 1, 1995, and announced that Essex Hemphill had passed away from AIDS. We had a moment of silence.

The Black queer men who were creating this lifesaving work were dying as we watched their films and read their books.

Marlon, I saw your work for the first time in Gary Lemmons's Black Masculinities at the Margins class. 1995, New York.

Teachers never know where their work will take them.

Marlon, you were dying as I was being born
Marlon, I could be wrong, but no one I knew back then called you disabled.

(Clip of Barbara Christian talking: "The last time I saw Marlon was at the party at the Pacific Film Archives ... and I have to say that I was shocked to see the way he looked. And yet there was still ... that calm, that patience, that certain quality of him really looking at you. He really looked at you. Even as he knew, I'm certain, that it was very difficult for those of us who had known him to look at him ... he looked at you.")

Marlon, it was so hard for me to look at this part of the video. These people, your queer Black and of color feminist peers, saying that it was so hard for them to look at your sick, disabled body.

You looked at them anyway.

And I am glad you looked anyway. But I want more.

A queer femme of color disabled artist elder friend of mine once talked about how the 1980s and 1990s AIDS movement was so clearly a disability movement. People were sick and struggling with the medical-industrial complex, getting drugs, surviving, changing bodies, needing help. People organized care teams and shifts to bring each other food and medicine. It was a movement of care and rage. But almost nowhere did AIDS movements think of themselves as disability movements.

I look at your peers looking away with distaste at your sick body, that they cannot see as strong and free. And it reminds me of the ways I have seen many of my able-bodied queer people of color looking away with distaste at the bodies of disabled and sick queer people of color—as we get sick. as we need things. as we can't go out, go out differently, ask for help. Require ASL or a ramp or no chemicals. At the ways people have looked away with distaste at my body as I use my cane. Have to stay home. Struggle for words. Need help with stairs.

It's really simple. My vision of freedom?

My vision of freedom is one where we are not abandoned.

Marlon, I look at you in your bed all femme Black sick queer and free, directing all your movies with ten fucking T cells from a hospital bed. You are a vision of what queer of color disabled genius artistry looks like. And my cells breathed it in years before I got sick.

Also you were funny as hell:

(History of Black music clip where Marlon dramatically acts out different Black musical genres in hospital gown, in hospital bed.)

And you changed everything. And you passed on into the other world.

(Clip of Alice Walker at Marlon's memorial: "He needed his feet massaged ... and Karen, who was up here earlier, took one foot, and I took the other, and we gradually worked on these feet and legs 'til he fell asleep. Now the gift of this, I'm still learning, because in this time when we can do nothing else—and it's such a horrible time—we can massage the feet of those who stand for us.")

We can massage the feet of those who stand for each other, sit for us, roll for us.

Marlon

I see all these abled people writing and speaking about how freaked out they were at seeing your disabled genius body.

I see you directing your last film from bed.

I see you sick and disabled queer Black genius dying free.

We can massage the feet of the people who stand for us.

This is my vision of freedom: that we can massage the feet of those who make us live. That we massage each other's feet. That we don't forget to remember our queer disabled Black and brown genius legacies. That we can make a movement where your memory makes us not abandon those of us who are sick.

You are still here.

(Closing clip of Marlon's voice saying, "Death can be transcended by memory. These people aren't dead to me. When I read about their lives, when I see their images in photos, I don't see death—I see this extremely empowering, life-giving force, and I know that I can achieve that too, and pass that on."

Images of Harriet Tubman, Martin Luther King, Sojourner Truth, Zora Neale Hurston, Frederick Douglass appear in a montage. Marlon's face is the last, placed among them as a beloved ancestor.)

6. cripstory

Cripstory

Commissioned in 2015 by the Paul K. Longmore Institute on Disability for their Patient No More *exhibit on the Section 504 protests.*

time doesn't move. we move through time.
—gabriel teodros

you're six and your mom has polio, but she won't talk about it
and you know you're a freak, but you don't talk about it either.
and you don't read in history class about crips
who locked down a building that says it wants to help us and we say it's
    saying fuck you to us.
no one tells you about a communist Mexican femme artist who paints her
    back brace and makes out with chavela vargas
you don't read about the freak show, the ugly laws,
the million indigenous words for disability that have nothing bad in them.
you just know your brain is weird and you can't ride a bike and you fall
    down in the shower
and get sick all the time and see visions. you're lucky to have bad HMO
    health insurance.
cripstory.

no one tells you that sick and disabled folks like lions make history. your
mom is busy passing as fuck. when you are 21 she'll say, *you know I had
polio. right? you know I can't walk down the street more than 30 feet without
pain right?* you don't/know she is surviving the best she can, by faking it,
something she'll teach you. you are both making history. two disabled

femmes, one white and straight and workingclass, one brown and queer and workingclass, surviving. cripstory.

it's not safe for you to be soft. to ask for things. you run away, an achy-hipped femme on the bus. you're making history. ten years later you see a queer/disabled porn made by a white queer femme in a wheelchair having sex in the disabled stall and waiting for the accessible bus the way you pray for a seat in the crip zone. you stammerstutter at her, run away, become friends. she invites you to a queer disabled sex performance night. you think it will be depressing. by the third act you are tearing up and rewriting your piece, your mouth open, turns out the d-word can mean joy. you're making history.

And when you're in high school ADAPT locks down their wheelchairs and scooters in front of buses and trains who are violently apologetic no room for us. *cripstory*.

in 2002 disabled queer people of color who will be your friends call out the white disabled queer conference on racism and make a zine. *cripstory*.

in 1993 your friend gets a double amputation after they get run over the first time they train hop. in 1994 their tiny zine, *ring of fire*, about queer and crip and genderqueer, doing drag while amputee, falls into your 19-year-old hands. Twenty-five years later you meet at a sins invalid show. you go to brunch, talk about your crip sex moments, collaborate in art and love. they go to speak to the nursing students about being disabled. teach crips at their physical rehab job how to fuck, love, be in their bodies. you move to their city. *cripstory*.

and when I was two years old, you all said fuck it and took over. you crawled. you made everyone stare 'cause everyone already stared anyway. you crawled up that flight of stairs because that's what rehab wanted you to do. crawl. because what else could you do but crawl. because we know crawling as art. as just another way our disabled bodies know how to move. took over that building that never helped us. made out with each other. made love. made history.

crip carnival. the opposite of the nursing home. you got free. *cripstory.*

we don't know what we give birth to. we don't know what just keeping breathing as disabled folks will do. we're not supposed to give birth. our genes are dangerous. but we do.

we are dangerous when we find each other. at the bottom of the stairs. in the crip seats. in the waiting room at kaiser or acupuncture. on tumblr. we are dangerous. all these points of cripstory like stars in the sky. you didn't know what you would give birth to. occupying the department of rehab. making out reaching to us almost forty years later. all our sweet drooling brokenbeautifulugly danger. a cosmos of crip story, all these moments, stars in the disabled genius sky.

For the Section 504 and Medicaid warriors and the Harriet Tubman Collective

Sri Lankan disabled futures 2017

thangatchi FB messages me drunk post the obligatory family visit from a hill station, promises me tea and arrack care package mailed from backhome. Says, what do you need more, tea or whiskey? These are the two brown liquids that traverse oceans and islands on small boats through currents to every place we end up. Somehow we often end up near water, ocean, great lakes, a shitty canal, a railroad that feels like an iron horse that flows like water.

I say, tea, Dilmah, export package. It's a brand that says it's a worker-owned co-op with pictures of smiling Tamil women plucking green leaves in the mountains we call hills, supposedly they have health insurance and profit sharing. it's kind of true, kind of a lie. it's good tea. thangatchi is too busy surviving brooklyn, as an immigrant come back to a month's jet-lagging to Trump and everyone else's america, to remember to or deal with making it to the post office, but I know the tea is there. That's enough.

I am a believer in possibility and I am a believer in dusty-booked history and mumbled drunk dad basement stories and feelings I couldn't prove when I finally hustled my way to see my grandparents' graves in Melbourne, not in Homebush but Box Hill, one of the first places Asian migrants landed in the '80s, and eager drunk fast-talk with other second-gen Lankan girls, tears and shrieks of laughter and family secrets and the healing power of kottu rotty.

I know we already died. I know the terror of the breaking. I know the portuguese, the dutch, the british and the world bank and the sinhalese nationalists all fucked us. I know terrible story after story. I know the vast archive of what has been forgotten and what is in languages I can't read.

I know I am here.

What I hold in my hands to offer you is this: green leaves, fast water, small boats, rushing. Someday I want to offer you the conversations had about our East African and Malaysian and Tamil Nadu and Filipinx cousins. I want a future where the Laccadive Sea, the Gulf of Aden, the Arabian Sea. The Red Sea and the Adamans are their own center of the world again, we sail those currents and the United States is a nightmare that we woke up from, fading away, where we are each other's reference point and white ableist colonialism is a scar being remediated.

I bequeath my legacy of faith in everything unexpected and wondrous. Everything Sri Lankan. Aren't we geniuses of the unexpected, we never expected any of this, the four colonial invaders, the tsunami wave, now the fake buddhist temples in the north and our marketing as the new Goa, we are experts at the you-can't-make-this-shit-up Lankan shrug, we didn't anticipate all the deaths or us not electing the asshole again or him coming back like Rasputin, the two queer women in love in the village buried together, the transformative justice healing rituals of Pattini-Kannaki?

I time travel and I see a future that is cripped the fuck out. Maybe what we do will not just change our lives? What if everyone is disabled in 2118? What if there are decked-out shower chairs and grab bars everywhere and stairs live in a museum? What if perfume is an ancient hate crime? What if we remade the world, it's normal and joyous to run a bag of IV antibiotics on a first date, text is everyone's first language they're never shamed out of, there are places to stim on every street corner in tiny libraries of joy? What if our island was a model?

What if our recombinant bodies, our lurches, our Crazy brilliant ideas solve all the unsolvable problems just by virtue of all the time we have to sit around? What if we solve the disposability crisis because all of us have been disposed of, we know how to medically advocate and do food drop-offs for even the people who annoy and piss us off the most?

Crip bodyminds live in beds and stars and I will hyperfocus my wild mind dreaming to find you.

The burning house

When you walk out of the burning house alive
the house will crumble and blow away
and no one but you will remember that it was on fire.
They will say there was never any house there,
they will change the subject.
You will be the only one who smells ash on your skin
using lungs scarred by breathing flame,
and still breathing.
They will call you crazy and oversensitive
when your wounds glow and burn.
when you refuse to cosmetic surgery your scars
when there is no technology that would cover them anyway

When you walk out of the burning house
you are the one who carries the gift of ashes
you are the one whose lungs are scarred strong by the memory of flame
The heatburn on your skin will glow when you sense others' wound
Your skin puckered, hypersensitive to touch:
you will remember, remember, remember.

Crip infinity

If my cane is a limb,
Then so is my pen
—Maranda Elizabeth

1. my friend asked her facebook feed what apocalypse would be too much
for us. What we would really want to not live beyond. Folks mentioned
cannibalism, the end of the whales, I stubborn said *nothing*.

I already died three times and came back
I trust this world's mean gorgeous unrelenting surprise
Like the best top,
she's taken me to the edge of death
and brought me back
over and over, transformed.
but if this world was sterile scrubbed held down of crip genius
I would not want to survive that
I would not want to live in a world where my people had been eliminated
for our own good.

2. in the infinite crip crazy future, I am not eliminated
and neither are you. We stand sit lie limp freak out
infinite.
There are kinds of crazy that we ain't even thought of yet.
We are the walking dead the dead femmes walking

There's nowhere you can hide from seeing all these birth defects,
I mean *people*   I mean us.

We really are everywhere
puffing, drooling, stimming.
The quality of our pain has changed
because no shame is the most effective anti-inflammatory

When an autistic kid is born people jump up and down
and scream quietly, in our heads. We are so excited to find out
what we can do.

The best stim toys and futures are made by our kind
who focused and focused and focused
'til we made something the most beautiful
and everyone gasped with admiration
but never surprise

Nothing horrible happens.
You are not taken away.
I am not left to die.
We take care of each other forever.

Our crip femme brown love is something studied in school
How we loved towards each other, again and again
—how a million ideations couldn't end this
We are an epic love story
We are one of many

All of us are worthy of study and grants, in fact
I don't mean the abled studying us
We study ourselves,
we check each other out in the mirror.

We are the beauty standard.
We didn't end.
Our wild minds make the future

I not in need of a cure

I my own amazing future

and yes, I ask:

what will we know about the queer crip body?
what do we know about the divine?
Persistent like virus
and as holy

3 crazy queens

1. **Nicole Demerin**, 1960–December 15, 2002

There is no Wikipedia entry for you. No Google image search hits. Less than three pages of scanty search engine replies documenting your life, your artwork, your crappy secretarial day job. Nicole, I couldn't find your obituary for a long time. When I ran into your old friend on the street in 2005 and he told me that you'd died, I think he just said some bullshit about how your fat had given you a heart attack. No one said maybe you died just because that's a thing bodies do, or that you died from a stressed-out survivor fat femme raised-poor broken heart.

You existed in a time before the assumption of digital recording everything. Yet you happened. Your existence is recorded in my body's archive, an archive of one crazy survivor femme who kept another one alive, one more important than anything the cloud can muster.

Nicole Demerin picked me up, nonsexually, outside a clinic defense some-where in the east 30s in Manhattan on a sunny September morning in 1993. I had just gotten out of my parents' house on a full ride, and I didn't go to sleep before 6 a.m. that whole year. I was out of lockdown family. On the streets. Hallucinating post–smoking a joint dosed with PCP at my high school graduation. Knowing I could tell no one about the panic attacks that were lasting days, hell, maybe they were one continuous panic attack my whole first year of college—if I did, I'd lose the scholarship, the ticket out of my abusive parents' house, I would be sent home and I would never be allowed to leave that Grey Gardens reality. I was running wild. A newly freed, feral ragtag crazy femme with $766 in a savings account from her mini-mart job, in a New York that had not yet been taken over by Giuliani and pasteurized.

So of course I was with all the other scholarship queer kids, shoplifting Tofutti from the bodega, trying to get into queer bar after bar without ID. Of course I hadn't slept. Of course when I pounded on all my friends' doors they didn't answer and I went to the clinic defense alone.

"You can totally have a cigarette, but they're Newports. Still want one, honey?" Nicole's voice was something between a husk and a screech with a lot of breathiness and a little caw like a crow. She was this weird fat femme in all stretchy black clothes, green sparkle glasses, braids crossed and pinned on her head. I thought she was white, but an internet search in 2017 reveals that 95% of everyone with the last name Demerin is Filipinx. She got my life story out of me and told me all of hers, with lots of screeching laughter and nonstop speedy talk, and in the end said, "I think you should come home with me! Just go grab a bag and take the N train—N for Nicole. Here's my address."

Nicole, you died December 15, 2002, at the age of 42, the age I am now.

You were only 15 years older than me when you revolutionary queer
    mothered me.
Invited me home. Bought takeout for both of us and shrugged away my
    attempts to give you $5.

You never tried to fuck me, although you absolutely supported my 18-year-old desires to fuck whoever I wanted. In fact, the whole year in you and your husband Keith's messy house, crowded with boxed-up shows, takeout containers, ashtrays, jazz CDs, nail polish, futons and weed, the spare room with a window facing a million pigeons on a shit-encrusted fire escape where I slept many nights, no one ever tried to fuck me. You taught me that takeout, smokes and cabs were crazy femme necessities that others would call luxuries, stupid girl things stupid girls blew their money on, but that cabs that were warm and food that came to your house were miracles.

You and all your 30something AIDS activist bisexual ex-junkie art friends were so kind to me it breaks my heart to remember it. You weren't afraid of being accused of corrupting a minor, you weren't trying to be homonormative because nothing like that existed yet, no one could get married or wanted to, you were sluts and junkies and survivors and AIDS nurses and artists. You probably had someone who had saved you, too. Or you wish you had. Your house was the first place I ever felt safe.

I've been thinking a lot about disability stories I didn't know were disability stories lately. Maybe it's not true that I didn't meet any other crips I could relate to 'til I was 31 and living in Oakland. Maybe we were passing disabled femme survivor knowledge back and forth on your couch, Nicole, in 1994. Because you were nuts and "annoying" to people because of it and you were very 1,000% open about having been molested by your stepfather, Jack, and pimped out by him and your mom and having run the fuck away to the Lower East Side.
You curated feminist and AIDS art shows at fancy spaces and squatter punk spaces on your couch, with cable blaring, takeout and your one hitter next to you, and me not able to get a word in edgewise.

You did shit that most social workers will never figure out, like that cigarettes and weed were safer drugs for my anxiety than first-generation Prozac would've been. That you gave me a task—a task!—that you knew I'd love and be good at, making the zine table at the show, and you told me I'd done such a good job and you were proud of me. You knew that if you treated me like I was competent and capable of making my own decisions as a batshit crazy 18-year-old, treated me with respect, took me with you in cabs to after-hours clubs and Sapphire poetry readings, talked to me survivor to survivor, showed me your art about the divine monstrous feminine and how to shoplift art supplies from work, that I would heal, or at least know I was loved.

You did shit in 1994 that predated all the Tumblr hard femmes by 20 years. Your hashtags would have been *Femme, bad girl, monstrous, goddess, danger, death, seduction, transgression, taboo feminine, power images of women confronting the viewer, eating you alive.*

Nicole, what would you tell me about surviving this world? *Make art on your couch with your bitches to survive the apocalypse. How do you think the best art gets made? Talking shit and screeching is medicine. Invite everybody centering the messiest. It can be worth it to force the big daddies in the big galleries to care about you, but you can make shit that saves lives in art shows, in squats and bodegas. Don't fuck the youth or fuck them over. Hold them like a tender baby bird heart, like your vulnerable survivor heart was and is.*

God is found in the heart of a messy raging monstrous survivor femme.
   Including yours.

2. **Marsha "Pay It No Mind" Johnson**, August 24, 1945–July 6, 1992

The ADA says that places of employment are required to make "all reasonable accommodations."
When you're mad, you are not reasonable.
Your brain is the opposite of reason.
So who accommodates us?

Marsha, I stand in the New Museum twenty years after the brief window
where we were both alive in this city.

I used to visit the piers where queer kids of color fucked and lived in
    cardboard houses
There was still safety on the edges.
The city still left the edges alone
The piers were not yet renovated into a dog park
It was unsafe and wonderful
I read *Transgender Warriors* from the library alone in my bed and learned
    about you.

Now, I see the film *Tourmaline* made of you, Mya playing you, reading a
poem in the club, "I could be loyal to the girls in the club not the cop on
the beat ..." cutting in with archival VHS of you going "Oh yeah, Stonewall!
I did start that! And then well ... I got lost in the music."

Lost in the music

is it ok to be disabled
is it ok to be nuts

reasonable accommodations
what if you do not hold Reason?

Marsha P. Johnson was nuts
would you be annoyed by her?
She's in the hospital AGAIN?
I care, I just have to have limits, you know?

who is crazy enough
to create and wear a flower crown every day when she has no house
to throw the first brick
in a cops face
defy Reason
demand the unreasonable
start every moment of queer liberation that has allowed my life?

if Marsha was here/Marsha is here
do you know
how
to love her?

Marsha would say
I wouldn't have made the revolution
if I wasn't crazy
Love the crazy queens in your midst
Listen to them
Love yourself

3. Taueret Davis, March 15, 1987–March 18, 2015

I open the queer of color tarot my love got me for solstice and there you
are, the Two of Wands. And I cry. I trace your face, say, *it looks just like*
her. Second-guess myself because after all, I wasn't your best friend or your
lover or a close companion, do I have a right to feel this or any way, to
mourn you.

I was just a brown femme in a circle of femmes coming together in the
early to mid-2000s, making zines, going to femme con. We circled each

other, admiring, keeping distant. So many things keep us from getting closer, doing more than saying hi at events, liking things on FB. When I visited Brooklyn I went to Re/Dress, the fat femme vintage store you worked at, you had an unerring eye and you picked out pieces for me, like you did for every Black and brown femme you loved. It was a way you showed us you loved us. Your burlesque name was Afrotitty, your aesthetic was a work of art. You were red lip, the word "cunty" two inches thick on a nameplate necklace, leopard print, good bourbon, unapologetic brat, getting what you wanted. You sold sex toys like many a queer at Babeland and then got a job teaching teen girls in a high school about sex, they loved you, *Miss T Miss T!*

When you were considering dying, I was one of the many sick and disabled femmes, so many Black and brown, who wrote back and forth to you on a 140-plus comment thread talking about our own dances with the other side, offering you places to stay, options, stories. In the end, you outsmarted everyone—if that's the right word. You went for exactly what you wanted and in the aftermath, like many femmes, I wonder, if queer community had been a place where messy, deeply depressed Black femmes were loved as unquestionably as your glinting performance self

if you knew you would be loved if you fell

held if you fell

respected and given autonomy if you needed to be held

would you still be here?

You are a new, recent ancestor.

The card's description says the Two of Wands learned everything she wanted to learn from this world. She stands there, asking you, *what is your deepest truth and desire, your deepest wound to heal?* Only facing those things in a world on fire will give you what you need to live. No small or easy task, but we are not a small or easy people. When I read from that deck, you are a guardian angel of Black and brown femmes considering suicide, popping up, perfect red lip, staring us in the eye, demanding that we not pretend things are fine or easy or ok. Demanding, in the middle of a world on fire, the deepest respect for our wound's telling.

Taueret says, *ask each other how you are doing, no, how are you really doing? See each other's beauty and adorn it for survival. Make homes and movements where mess is beloved.*

Litany

—after Audre Lorde

For all the ways we learned to mother ourselves
divinity, in small rooms
for all the ways we caught tears in rain barrels, clean water
made balm out of waste fryer oil and cedar
for all the ways no one taught us/we taught ourselves
out of our solar's best magnet,
for all the ways there are no cards or cakes for this labor
I say I treasure, witness and remember you, and the way
we survived who were never meant to survive.

because the sun comes up and we wish it would not return, but it does
because the sun goes down and we sigh with relief and terror
because the bed is too narrow and the walls are too wide
I cannot cross over.

Because the ways we reach to each other and fail are divinity
because I do not have more recent pictures than 1930 of my closest ancestors,
but I have their names written in colored pencil on my altar
because at my craziest I hear their roughsoft centralmass accents, urging
   me on, kid

I made myself medicine out of weeds and gave myself the respite house
that didn't exist of my own apartment
you sent me a million bitmojis telling me you loved me when neither of us
   could talk
I hear your guyanese british accent in every "my dear" on WhatsApp

you bought an air mattress and soft purple sheets and gave me keys with a
    sparkly gold circle
because you wanted me to know I always had a home with you

I taught myself words and manners, to smile at and treat everyone with
    respect
out of books and my friends, I taught myself to apologize,
most of all to myself.
You breathed and laughed me through every screaming panic attack and I
    returned the favor
you walked with me through the supermarket

My chest wall opens and this poem flies out of the muscle of my heart and
    bicep
you write a book about your parts and mine all open their mouths

for the endless cups of rose tulsi tea, the care packages across borders that
    cost $435 in postage
the handmade asshole repellant spray
and the faith
the sun goes up
the sun goes down
we are our own right to return

Photo: Jesse Manuel Graves

LEAH LAKSHMI PIEPZNA-SAMARASINHA is a queer disabled femme writer, cultural worker, organizer and educator of Burgher/Tamil Sri Lankan and Irish/Roma ascent. They are the author of *Care Work: Dreaming Disability Justice, Dirty River: A Queer Femme of Color Dreaming Her Way Home* (shortlisted for the Lambda and Publishing Triangle Awards, ALA Over the Rainbow List), *Bodymap* (shortlisted for the Publishing Triangle Award), *Love Cake* (Lambda Literary Award winner), and *Consensual Genocide,* and coeditor of *The Revolution Starts at Home: Confronting Intimate Violence in Activist Communities.* With Ejeris Dixon, they are the coeditor of *This Is How We Survive: A Transformative Justice Reader,* forthcoming in 2019. A lead artist with Sins Invalid and cofounder of the queer and trans people of color performance collective Mangos With Chili from 2006 to 2015, her writing has been widely published, with recent work in PBS NewsHour, Poets.org's *Poetry and the Body* folio, *The Deaf Poets Society, Bitch, Self, TruthOut* and *The Body Is Not an Apology.* She is a VONA Fellow and holds an MFA from Mills College. She is also a rust belt poet, a Sri Lankan with a white mom, a femme over forty, a grassroots intellectual, a survivor who is hard to kill. Follow Leah at *brownstargirl.org.*